D1601298

If I'm So Free~ How Come I Feel Boxed In?

Also by Dr. Guernsey . . .
Thoroughly Married

If I'm So Free~ How Come I Feel Boxed In?

Dennis Guernsey

WORD BOOKS
PUBLISHER
4800 WEST WACO DRIVE
WACO, TEXAS
76703

Library of Congress Catalog Card Number: 77-92449
ISBN 0-8499-0066-2

Printed in the United States of America

To
SHERYL AND SHANNON

It is a delight to be their father
and their zest for life is my clearest example
of what it really means to be free.

Contents

Preface

Several years ago in graduate school I became fascinated with the emerging ideas of self–concept and self–image. I remember driving home on the freeway with my mind traveling even faster as I meditated upon the implications of what I had just heard that day about human personality. Even more vividly, I remember thinking how important it would be for the body of Christ to be exposed to the same information. I covenanted with myself to write a book about the subject as soon as I found time. Quite to my surprise, within a few months I saw "my book" advertised in a Christian periodical under someone else's name and under another title! I couldn't believe my eyes. The author had written exactly the book I wanted to write. He had beat me to the punch. "Oh, well," I rationalized, "I'll just have to write about something else."

My next area of inspiration was the Christian family. I had dedicated myself to the task of studying the Christian family, and I was sure I had found my niche. No sooner had I settled into my doctoral studies on the family when hundreds of books about the Christian family began to tumble off the printing presses. The Christian world was deluged with material on the very topic I had committed myself to study. I was a day late and a dollar short again.

When I finally found time to write my first book, *Thoroughly Married*, published by Word Books, I was sure its subject matter would be pristine in the sense that very few Christian books had dealt with the subject of sexuality in Christian marriage. It shouldn't have surprised me, but no sooner was my first book off the presses than it was joined on the shelves of bookstores by a score of books with similar emphasis. I was no longer behind the times—I was running neck and neck.

As for the book now before you, I have allowed myself no illusions whatsoever. I fully expect it to be met on the shelves of Christian bookstores with fellow titles designed to speak to the same issue of Christian freedom. Why? Because every age has its "catch words" and the idea of "freedom" is a word that has reached its time. The Germans have a concept that roughly translates into the "spirit of the times." It means that certain ideas seem to wrap up the concerns and thinking of an age better than others. The spirit of the time involves what catches the attention of the authors and readers of a given generation. The idea of "freedom" is just such a word. It is an idea that seems to hover above most of our lives, just out of reach. I am convinced it was an idea that filled the minds of the first century Christians as well. What does it mean to be free? How does one gain that inner sense of personal freedom for which we all seem to hunger?

At this juncture it's appropriate to mention the real

heroes of this book. Its pages are filled with the experiences of many who have become my dearest and closest friends, friends who have journeyed with me in the search for the freedom that Jesus gives. I hope I have been able to mask and mute the specifics of the case histories involved. Usually I have combined several similar cases into one in the hope that anonymity will be preserved. If my patients or my friends recognize themselves it is because their struggles have been so much a part of mine. Much of the time they have been my teachers. Their experiences with the attending pain and struggle have forced me to reevaluate my thinking, my ministry, and in many cases, my life itself. I am deeply appreciative of their patience and perseverance.

Jesus said as a part of the spirit of his times, "If the Son therefore shall make you free, ye shall be free indeed" (John 8:36). What concerned him then concerns many of us today. We thirst for a taste of the freedom he offered but in searching we sometimes miss, only to go on searching. This book is simply meant to help those of us who are searching to be free. In Christ we are meant to be "free indeed." The question then comes, "If I'm so free, how come I feel boxed in?"

1

Free to Love Yourself

Free to Love Yourself

A couple of years ago my family and I had gone to my in-laws' house to celebrate my birthday. My brother-in-law had just purchased a new motorcycle, and I decided to try it out. I hopped on the machine and took off, not realizing that it was much bigger and more powerful than any I had ever ridden. Also, in my haste I failed to put the helmet on, a deadly mistake. Less than two houses away I rounded the corner and hit a small puddle of water—and the bike began to slide. As I touched the throttle just a little to straighten the bike up, I hit it more than I realized because the machine responded with a roar and pointed me at a parked car. In my panic I decided to lay the bike down in the middle of the street rather than hit the car. The bike and I collided with the pavement going about twenty or so miles an hour. I flew off and sprawled face first. When the arms and legs and wheels stopped I was a mess, and the bike was, too. I got up and started walking back. By this time the whole family had emptied out of the house and had come running to my aid. My wife led me into the bathroom and began to clean me up. A brief examination convinced her that I needed to go to the hospital.

At the hospital the nurses in the emergency room took the information and parked me in a room to wait for the doctor. When he finally came he looked at me and shrugged knowing that before him lay one of the most fortunate people in the world. I agreed with him completely. He washed me off and stitched me up and then sent me on my way with a short but gentle lecture about the dangers of motorcycles. I believed every word and took a vow never to ride on one again. The ride back to the house was quiet as we all contemplated how fortunate I was. We finished my birthday celebration somewhat hurriedly, and I went home to begin my period of recuperation. That night I went to bed bandaged but whole, thankful and wiser.

The next morning I awoke but couldn't open my right eye. For a moment I couldn't figure out what was wrong. Then I looked over at my wife with my good eye and said something. The look on her face told me everything I needed to know. My face was terribly swollen, and I was horrible to look at. Try as she might she couldn't keep from recoiling at the sight. I had yet to see myself in a mirror, but I knew full well what I looked like. I could see myself clearly in her response to me. A quick look in the mirror corroborated the bad news. My face was a mess. Fortunately, within a few days the swelling was gone and my features returned to normal, but I'll never forget the look in Lucy's eyes when she saw me. And I'll never forget the sinking feeling inside me when I realized what I must have looked like.

I've begun this chapter on loving yourself with this

personal illustration because it points out a significant fact essential to my treatment of the subject. I knew what I looked like after my accident without seeing myself by "seeing" myself in my wife's response to me. So it is with how we come to "see" ourselves inside. All that we really know about ourselves as people is what we've experienced in the responses of others to us, especially the significant others.

Seeing Myself

I carry a picture of myself around inside of me, a picture created brush stroke by brush stroke by those who have touched my life from the time I was a small child. The brush strokes painted on the canvas of my life when it was clean and uncluttered are the strokes that are the most significant. My mother, my father, my brothers, and sisters, as well as any other person or persons who walked around in my early life, each left their imprints on my view of myself. Their imprints were left in the form of their responses to me. Psychologists refer to this as "self–image," or "self–concept." The idea of "self" is key to an understanding of what this chapter is all about. Each of us has formed some kind of "inner" picture. That picture is strongly influenced by the significant others in our early life.

Suppose you were to imagine yourself as you were when you were about four years old, just before you went off to school for the first time. Remember the house or apartment you lived in. Try to remember as many of the details as you can. What did the front of the house look like? What about the back? The kitchen? Your bedroom? Where did you spend most of your time? Now remember that place and let the memories filter down through the years and into the present.

Try to remember all of the people who slept at your house at that time. Remember them by name. Your parents, your brothers and sisters, if you had any, and any others who would have touched your life. Picture each of them in your mind.

The next step is to imagine in your mind that it's early one Saturday morning and you're the first one up. Let yourself bounce out of bed. One at a time walk into the bedroom of the others in your family. Reach out, touch their shoulders, and wake them up.

—What is the look you see in their faces? Are they glad to see you or are they angry? What response do you see in each of their faces?

—What do they say to you? Are you welcome or unwelcome? Are you friend or foe? What's the tone of their voices? Are they harsh—or soft and gentle? Do you belong there—or are you an intruder?

—What are you feeling as you stand in front of each of them? Are you comfortable or uncomfortable? At ease or ill–at–ease?

If you have allowed yourself the freedom to remember you are beginning to catch a glimpse of your "self–concept," the early memories of others' responses to you. If you have trouble remembering, it may be because you are protecting yourself from the unpleasantnesses of unhappy memories. Whatever your

18

memories, the responses of those significant people form the basis upon which you built your "self–image." You can't get away from it. You have a "self–image," and that's where it all began.

My Self-Image

It's impossible to overestimate how influential those early memories are and how they affect us today. It may well be that your memories were all warm and good and affirming. So much the better. For some of us, however, the memories are painful and the images we see of ourselves are twisted and distorted. If that's the case for you, probably one of two outcomes have resulted. Either you still carry the distortions around inside you as the residue of your past, or you have spent much of your adult life overcoming those images.

If you are one of those who still carries the distortions around as part of your present day self–image, you typically hear one of two messages. In the first place, when you hear others responding to you positively, you, in response, may find yourself disclaiming their opinions. You find it extremely difficult to accept or even hear compliments. You've never in your life been able to respond to a compliment by saying, "Thank you. That feels good." You get caught on that merry–go–round of wanting the compliments, and even, at times, soliciting them, while at the same time discounting them when they come and feeling somehow guilty when someone responds to you favorably.

The second typical response of those who carry the distortions of the past around as part of their self–image is the response that begins with the presupposition that the other guy in any conversation is wrong and you're right. "Why try to get along with him because he probably won't like me—so why try?" If this is your pattern, you're probably accused of being argumentative and defensive much of the time, even to the point of having a reputation for being hard to get along with.

The response for many of us to the distortions of the past is to live out our adult lives with a "I can't be that bad, it must be you" kind of attitude. We seem to carry a chip around on our shoulder and it feels like others are continually trying to knock it off. Though we don't like to admit it, down deep inside we've come to realize that the problems in our relationships are probably ours more often than not. It scares us to death to admit it. This response is an uncomfortable place to be— both for the person who carries that image around inside and for those with whom he or she lives. The answer to the dilemma is to do something about your self–image, the way you feel about yourself inside. What you can do about it is to learn to love yourself, to gain a different opinion about yourself, to redefine the images from the past to fit another set of images in the present.

One of the incredible advantages of having a personal relationship with God through his Son Jesus Christ is that *in Christ each of us has the opportunity to reconstruct the images of the past.* It well may be that the early responses of significant others to me have provided me with a set of distorted images of myself. However, in Christ I have had provided for me a new set of mirrors. I have an alternative. I can live and think of myself in terms of the past, or I can live and think of myself as I am in Christ. How I make that choice determines to a large extent whether I am "free indeed." Learning to love yourself is part of that freedom.

What Loving Yourself Isn't

Before I begin to define for you what I think it means to love yourself, it's important that I define what loving yourself isn't.

To begin with, *loving yourself isn't selfishness.* It is, in fact, just the opposite. An illustration might be helpful. Suppose by some stroke of luck I learn there is to be a sugar shortage. My response to the news is to hustle down to the local supermarket to stock up on sugar. As I come up to the check–out stand the checker comments that someone at my house must really like sugar. Little does she know that I have anticipated the demand and have secured enough sugar to last me for a year.

The question that is relevant is, does the sugar hoarder's behavior prove anything about his attitude toward sugar? The answer is obvious. You can only understand the hoarder mentality, that is his selfishness, if you understand that he believes there's going to be a sugar shortage. From his point of view, there will not be enough sugar to go around. This kind of selfish

21

behavior occurs when the person becomes convinced the supply of a particular commodity is insufficient for the demand and that he'll be on the short end of the supply.

So it is with the selfish person. He is convinced there will be a shortage of the commodity in question. If left to the natural consequences of life he will be left out. No one will see to it that he will be cared for. He must look after his own interests because no one else will.

In contrast, the person who genuinely loves himself isn't preoccupied with shortages. If there's not enough, he'll get by. He operates on the assumption that his needs will be met. He's secure in and of himself. Take Jesus Christ, for instance. He operated under the assumption that his Father would meet his needs and because of that assumption he could give himself away. The selfish person operates under the opposite assumption. He must take care of himself because no one else will. You can only love yourself if you're secure in the love of someone else.

Not only is loving yourself not selfishness, *it's also not show–offishness.* The same reasoning as in the case of the hoarder holds true here. Suppose I walk into a room and immediately begin to draw attention to myself. I'm louder than anyone else. I'm more dramatic. I seem to need to dominate the attention of everyone in the room. Is my behavior an indication that I love myself? No, it isn't. It is probably an indication that I really believe I must draw attention to myself, or no one will notice me.

This fact was driven home to me in one of my

graduate classes in psychology. Our assignment was to observe a fifth grade class in one of the local elementary schools. We were to observe the behavior of the children and then try to identify which of the children would score the highest on a measurement of self-esteem. Carefully observing my class, I then recorded my opinions. I chose the boy who seemed to tower above the others with his presence. He seemed to be the most verbal, the most intelligent, and by far the most dominant.

Much to my complete surprise when the results of the self-esteem measurements were available, the boy I nominated was one of the lowest in the class. The child with the highest was a plain little girl who seemed on the surface to be extremely shy. I couldn't believe the results until I returned to the classroom and watched the children in action the next day. My observations this time confirmed the accuracy of the test. The shy little girl always had someone standing by her desk talking to her. When the children went out to play, the other girls in the class wanted to play with her. When it was lunch time they ate with her. She was in the center of the group but most of the time she said very little. And, when it came time to leave for home, two of her friends ran halfway across the playground to walk with her. She was one of the quietest and most unassuming of the children but she obviously was one of the best liked. This little girl was at ease with herself.

This is not to say that only shy children love themselves. I'm just saying that personality factors such as introversion and extroversion have little to do with loving yourself. It is possible to love yourself and at the same time be quite shy or be quite outgoing. Loving yourself means you don't have to draw attention to yourself. You operate under the assumption that others will notice you in due time. It's an issue you don't have to worry about. The cream will always rise to the top.

What Loving Yourself Does Mean

Having discussed what loving yourself does not mean, I now want to discuss what it does mean. I have found it useful to think of loving yourself as a three–dimensional concept. Loving yourself involves having a sense of personal worth, personal identity, and personal adequacy. The three key terms are worth, identity, and adequacy.

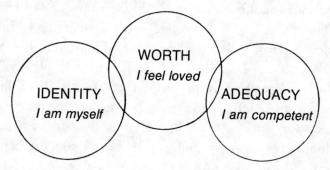

You can see in the above diagram that the concepts are interrelated with each other. Each circle touches the others signifying that each concept is connected with the others and they, in fact, have a common dimension. Loving yourself is a combination of components each contributing to the whole but none being equal to the whole.

Loving yourself, in the first place, involves a sense of personal worth. A sense of personal worth is the same as feeling loved, with the emphasis upon the *felt* love. It's one thing to say to yourself that you are loved and quite another to *feel* that you are.

I remember walking out of my office at a church where I once served only to see a little girl come skipping out of the church office on her way back to her classroom. Evidently, she had been sent on an errand by her day school teacher and she was reporting back to her class as ordered. The distance from the church office to her classroom was about 100 feet. As she skipped she chanted a little saying to keep herself in step. "My mommy loves me . . . my daddy loves me . . . my teacher loves me . . . my grandma loves me . . . God loves me . . . Jesus loves me . . . ." She *felt* loved, 100 feet worth. I continued on my way impressed with the privileged position of that little girl and how much I wished my patients felt just one–tenth of the love she felt. What a difference it would make in their lives.

I don't mean to imply in the above illustration that personal worth is a function of how many people love you either. The rule of thumb is, "I don't need to be loved by everyone. I just need to be loved by some-one." Personal worth grows to the degree I allow my-self to believe that a significant other loves me.

It is at this point that the love of God is so crucial. It well may be that as a child I grew up not feeling loved by anyone. The mirrors of my past are twisted and distorted to the point I feel emotionally ugly. What a contrast to see myself in the mirror God has provided for me. He loved me so much that he allowed his very own Son to die so that I might inherit eternal life. I must be of incredible worth to God. Even though I am a sinner, I am an object of his love, a love that involved the sacrifice of Someone he loved.

Why is it that we Christians find it so hard to bask in the love of God? It seems to me that sometimes we have become so preoccupied with the teaching of total depravity, the inherent sinfulness of man, that we begin to believe we are valueless. You just can't understand and experience the love of Christ if that's the case, if you have no value. Each of us must be of inestimable value to God. To diminish our value to him is to diminish the meaning and value of Christ's death.

Thus, the first step in coming to love myself is to look full into the mirror of God's responses to me. If the mirrors of my early childhood were clear and affirming, then God's response to me in Christ corroborates those messages. If the mirrors of my childhood were distorted, then God's mirror provides me with an alternative message. The ultimate decision is, which set of mirrors will I believe?

The second component in loving yourself is a sense of personal identity. When I use the concept of identity, I take it to mean a sense of "I am myself." There are dimensions of me as a person that are unique. I am unlike anyone else in this world. Those who suffer from a lack of personal identity think themselves to be fashioned according to someone else's mold. They are carbon copies of another's personality and opinions.

When I served on the staff of a large church I often brushed aside my wife's protestations that she was thought of as "Dennis Guernsey's wife," rather than as Lucy Guernsey. I was aware that many of my friends in the ministry had wives and children who resented that they were always thought of as the "pastor's wife" or the "preacher's kid." It didn't seem all that important to me. I wasn't aware of their feelings until the shoe was on the other foot.

After I had left my church responsibilities and had taken a job as the executive director of a Christian social service agency, for about three months I continued at our former church on Sundays while Lucy and the two children began attending our new home church. For three months every Sunday we went our separate ways. During those three months Lucy and the girls became totally involved in the life of the new church. By the time I finished my old responsibilities and began attending with them, I was greeted with, "Oh, you're Lucy Guernsey's husband." At first I jokingly shrugged it off but for months each time I would meet someone new I would be "Lucy Guernsey's husband." After a while it began to irritate me and then I remembered. For five years in my previous position I had been the one in our family who established our identity. Now, in this new social situation, Lucy had taken the lead in establishing our identity. It became an irritant that reminded me of my need for identity.

27

Rarely, if you're the dominant one who charts the course of your family's identity, are you aware that others in your family might chafe when they're referred to as so–and–so's husband or wife, or someone's little sister or kid brother. Each of us needs to feel a sense of individuality. We need to feel that when we take a step in the sand, our footsteps are left behind rather than someone else's. That's what personal identity is all about.

Where does personal identity come from? Personal worth results from feeling loved by both of your parents, whereas personal identity results, in the main, from the responses and messages of your opposite sexed parent. That is, mothers help sons to feel unique and special while fathers help daughters feel especially important. It is the parent of the opposite sex who establishes the sense of identity.

This is especially true in the case of our sexual identity, a sub–category of the general component of personal identity. One of the major responsibilities of a father is to help his daughter feel good about being feminine. Likewise, one of the major responsibilities of being a mother is to make your son feel good about his masculinity. How comfortable we feel about our sexuality is tied very strongly to the messages we received from our opposite sexed parent.

In one of the undergraduate classes I taught on marriage and the family I was pressed by the class to give suggestions having to do with mate selection. What criteria can you use when selecting a mate? In particular a young man in the back of the class was concerned about predicting sexual compatibility since he as a Christian had ruled out premarital intercourse. I thought about it a while and then responded with the suggestion that he observe the quality of relationship the girl had with her father. If it was warm and affectionate and she felt affirmed by him the odds were that she would be able to relate to her husband warmly and affectionately and the sexual relationship would follow right in line. There were other suggestions and the lecture on mate selection seemed to be the best remembered.

Three years later I saw that same young man in the seminary where I now teach. He came up to me following chapel one day and reminded me of the advice I had given the marriage and family class three years before. He had taken me seriously and had used my criteria in helping him select a mate. In particular, he remembered the suggestions I gave regarding sexual compatibility. He had applied them and had found a girl who fit all of his prerequisites in addition to having a warm and affectionate relationship with her father. He thanked me for the advice and with a parting shy glance he told me that their sexual relationship was all he had hoped it could be. It felt good to have my teachings affirmed in such a practical and livable way.

But what about those of us who had poor or conflicted relationships with our opposite sexed parent? Does this mean we're doomed to sexual purgatory? Certainly not. It only means that we have the additional responsibility of establishing our sense of personal identity on our own without the benefit of the affirming messages from father or mother. For some of us it means we have to undo their messages. For others of us it means that we have to look for other sources of responses in our search for identity.

Again, it is here that a personal relationship with Jesus Christ can make a difference. How? Through laying hold of a very basic principle of Scripture. Each of us has been created in the image of God (Gen. 1:26). When we come into a personal relationship with him through his Son, the fullness of his creation is restored. To say it another way, in Christ we reflect a unique facet of the nature and character of God. None of us is alike. We are all different and our God has numbered the hairs on our heads. He has catalogued us and he knows us as separate human beings. Our uniqueness can be, if we will allow it, the start of something good. Upon that uniqueness we can build a fully orbed sense of our own personal identity.

The third component of loving yourself is a sense of personal adequacy. While a sense of worth involves feeling loved, and a sense of identity involves feeling that you are a special, unique person, a sense of personal adequacy involves a feeling of competence. It is that inside part of the person that believes he or she can do what he has set out to do—or at least give it a good try.

Have you ever known someone who seems able to do almost anything? The nature of the task is irrelevant. What is relevant is his willingness to try new things, to risk being wrong because he always knows he can pull it off somehow. Loving yourself involves a feeling of personal sufficiency.

Where does this feeling come from? Personal worth is a gift of both parents; identity is a gift from the parent of the opposite sex; and a sense of personal adequacy, in the main, is a gift from the parent of the same sex. It is what is transmitted from fathers to sons and from mothers to daughters.

The specific content the father gives to his son really doesn't mean that much. Some fathers may give the ability to work on mechanical things, another father may give an ability to work with numbers, while still another may give an artistic sense or the ability to be creative or even domestic. The content of what is transmitted from the same sexed parent to his child is incidental to the transmission of the ability *to do* or *try* whatever is defined for the child. The psychological mechanism at work is probably the mechanism of identification, the tendency of a child to identify with the parent of the same sex.

But what about those of us who, for one reason or another, grew up feeling incompetent? Or in a single parent home? Is there any hope for us? Again, in loving yourself there is hope, and the ability to love yourself is strengthened by your relationship to God.

I think this facility of competence was the one that was the weakest in me as a young adolescent. My father had died when I was seven and my growing up years were pretty well dominated by women. My mother, my grandmother, and my aunts all tried hard to raise me. There was one thing they couldn't give me though. It was the ability to feel competent as a man. Most of my adolescent years were spent feeling desperately inadequate and lacking in basic maleness.

31

On a human level, it was competitive athletics (particularly football) that helped me feel better about myself as a man. The disciplines of the game brought a new dimension to my life. But there was still something missing. The ingredient of personal adequacy just wasn't there. It wasn't until I came into a personal relationship with Jesus Christ that this sense of personal adequacy began to grow. For the first time I had someone I could identify with. Jesus became the man in my life and his presence made a difference. For the first time I became willing to try new things, to go new places, and to risk failure. Just the simple knowledge that I wasn't alone really helped.

As I grew in my Christian life other dimensions of my relationship to Christ began to make a difference, especially the teaching in the New Testament regarding spiritual gifts. I came to realize that my early childhood might have been lacking as far as learning how to be a man was concerned, but that lack didn't mean a thing as far as my abilities and successes in the body of Christ were concerned. What mattered more was my spiritual gift and my willingness to allow the Lord Jesus to use me as he saw fit.

The concept of spiritual gifts involves several scriptural facts. First of all, it is a fact that each believer in Jesus Christ has been given at least one spiritual gift (1 Cor. 12:7). Secondly, this gift is sovereignly bestowed. That means that God is the giver and man is the receiver. It also means that these gifts are different from natural talents or abilities (also 1 Cor. 12:7). And thirdly, the gifts come in different sizes and shapes, depending upon the function of the gift in the body of Christ (Rom. 12, 1 Cor. 12, Eph. 4).

The practical result is that while I well may feel terribly inadequate when it comes to life in general, that needn't be the case if I am a part of the body of Christ. My ability to succeed in his body depends upon my gift or gifts. In that sense he is my source of adequacy.

The Difference It Makes

What a difference he made in my life. It was the difference between day and night. What has grown in me is the belief that I don't have to be afraid of failure or even the risk of failure. Admittedly, I still have problems with feeling inadequate about working on cars, or fixing up around the house. Those practical matters still haunt me. The sense of personal competence is more than the ability to perform particular skills, however. An inventory of my life to this point indicates that I have accomplished some very demanding tasks and that behind that accomplishment is belief in myself, a belief that came about because of my relationship with Jesus Christ. I look back on the day when as an eighteen-year-old I humbled my heart before God and invited Jesus Christ to be my Lord as being the day I became not only a Christian but also a whole person. "Old things were passed away and every thing became new" (2 Cor. 5:17).

There are many of us who have never in our entire lives even given thought to the idea that loving ourselves is important. Jesus said that we are to "love thy neighbor *as* *thyself*" (Matt. 22:39). I've already suggested earlier in this chapter that many of us have difficulty in getting along with people. There's something about us that just doesn't seem to fit. Maybe the missing ingredient is that we need to learn to be "free to love ourselves." If we learn this, then we'll like ourselves better and, just maybe, we'll be easier to live with. We'll have begun to taste what it means to be "free indeed."

2

Free to Serve One Another

Free to Serve One Another

In the course of a year I am often asked what problem do I most commonly encounter as a Christian therapist. The curiosity of the inquirer has usually been provoked by something I have said or something they have read. My answers to the questions have varied over the years to the point where I'm sure there isn't *one* most common problem but a cluster of related problems, especially when it comes to marriage.

I have come to one particular conclusion, however. It has to do with an issue I'm convinced lies at the center of many of the relational problems that exist between people. The major issues of life, I have become convinced, revolve around the issue of power, or control, or authority, or whatever you might call it. Who is going to control whom is a fundamental question underlying most relationships.

For example, it was the issue of control that formed the backdrop to the struggle between God and his archangel Lucifer, before he fell and became Satan, the god of this world. The same issue existed in the confrontation between Jesus Christ and Satan as it was played out in the wilderness—that is, who would control Jesus? It is the issue of power or control or authority that characterizes the struggles between political ideologies and nations at war. It is the need to resolve the same issue that is resident in each and every relationship between human beings. Who is going to control whom? When it comes to marriage, the issue is there, as it were, in bold letters.

Only recently has the issue come under open and public discussion. It is the issue between races, between the young and the old, and between the sexes. Who will rule or control whom? For centuries the issue has been resolved culturally through the bounds of tradition. It has been the tradition of centuries for the whites to rule the non–whites, for the old to rule the young, for the males to rule the females.

"Tradition," cried Tevye, in *Fiddler on the Roof.* It defines the rules of supremacy if you are on the top and it provides the chains of bondage if you are on the bottom. But since World War II we have experienced a series of revolutions as one suppressed minority or majority after another have asserted their independence and demanded their rights to be free, and in some cases their right to replace the rule of their oppressors with a rule of their own. Carried to the extreme it becomes, "You ruled us for centuries, now it's our turn to rule you."

I'm sure if you're the suppressed party this kind of reasoning makes sense. But, if you or your kind have been the suppressors and have been traditionally on the top, the logic ends right there. Suddenly, "two wrongs don't make a right." "Excesses in one direction don't excuse excesses in the other." When the shoe is on the other foot the pinch becomes something more than an academic debate. It becomes the fodder for real, blood–and–guts conflict.

The Marital Conflict

As the struggles over who will control whom have bubbled to the surface of the contemporary landscape, the issue of power and control seems to have become central in marital conflict as well. More and more "submissive" wives are challenging their traditional role. "Who says that I'm to be submissive?" "Why does it always have to come out the husband's way?" The reaction, rather than response, of the embattled male is too often one of rancor and bitterness. Jaws are set and necks stiffen as the lines of battle are drawn. Unfortunately, by the time the dust of battle settles the scars of war have seriously damaged the relationship, or at least it would appear so.

Just such a battle took place between my wife and myself a couple of years ago. It began a process that resulted in a fundamental change in my thinking about the husband–wife relationship. I have always prided myself on being what I thought was a "liberated male." Ours was an "equal" marriage, a partnership I said to myself and to others. I liked the sound of the words and I liked the avant–garde badge it seemed to give me. I wore the badge with pride until one evening when my opinions of myself were brought into question. The occasion was simple enough. Lucy, my wife, informed me that after twelve years of marriage she wanted to go back to work. She had worked full time until our first child was born and had worked part time on several occasions since. But this time was different.

The motivation wasn't simply our need for money as it had been before. This time she was restless and by her own words had begun to question her own worth. I liked having her home. She was *my* wife and the mother of *my* children and *I* liked the situation the way it was. Later I had to admit that I was operating under at least two false assumptions: first of all, that being a wife and a mother should be all that a woman needs to fulfill herself as a person, and secondly, that a husband should be able to fill all of his wife's needs and that if he hasn't there must be something wrong with him. Lucy's intention to return to work threatened my idyllic world and my inflated opinion of myself.

"No! I don't think that your going back to work would be a good idea," I answered even before she had finished her request.

"I'm sorry, what did you say?" she replied.

"I said you can't go back to work. I won't let you."

Her face reddened with frustration.

"I'm just trying to let you know that I'm feeling boxed in. I want to be part of the world again."

"I guess you didn't hear what I'm saying. I said No. There is such a thing as the chain of command, you know!" There—I had said it! I pulled rank on her. Now, I thought, she has to do what I said, because we both believe the Bible and after all it does say that wives are to "submit" to their husbands.

Rather than obedient submission, her response was something I wasn't ready for. She began to cry, burying her face in her hands and sobbing.

"You can't say that. I'm a person." Over and over she chanted the same thing. "I'm a person."

"For crying out loud. I'm not saying you're not a person. I'm just saying that I don't want you to go back to work." The tension between us was incredible. Suddenly I wanted to leave, so I told her I didn't want to talk about it any more. I stormed away muttering under my breath. Everything had gotten all turned around. I knew something was wrong but didn't know what.

Earlier that very evening I had been at a local church lecturing on the husband–wife relationship. I had pointed out that the marital relationship in many ways should reflect the kind of relationships that exists between the members of the Trinity. I had quoted Genesis 1:27 as my scriptural support.

"So God created man in his own image, in the image of God created he him; *male and female* created he them." The first marriage between Adam and Eve mirrored the relationships between the Godhead. I had said that the relationship between husband and wife is a relationship between equals, it's to be voluntary, that it is not coercive, and they are to be mutually submissive to one another. Submission is a two–way street.

Following our quarrel I had walked away no more than a few steps when my own words began to haunt me. "Voluntary and *not coercive.*" Just five minutes

41

earlier I had attempted to bully my wife into doing what I wanted her to do rather than allowing her to make up her own mind. For the life of me I couldn't imagine God the Father bullying the Son into doing anything. Whatever their relationship was, it didn't include treating each other in the way I had just treated my wife. I went to bed that night a troubled man.

The next morning I approached Lucy and apologized for my actions the night before. I tried to tell her why I was upset and that if she needed to go back to work, I would do what I could to help make it happen. Our relationship had been bruised but the battle was over. Four days later she had a job.

The next year or so was a real thrill for me. Lucy launched out into the business world and gradually her old confidence in herself began to return. She was a whole person who could function on her own. Her faith in Christ was real and she thrived on the challenges of a new and different environment. She was more than a wife and a mother. Lucy was a person in her own right. In fact, her discovery of her personhood helped her become a better wife and mother.

It was during that year I came upon a quote that was of inestimable help to me at the time.

"If you love something, set it free.
If it comes back, it is yours.
If it doesn't, it never was."

I had been afraid to set Lucy free. Unconsciously I think I was afraid she wouldn't really want me if she had a choice. It was my own insecurity that was getting

in the way. I had to let her go. To my great pleasure
once she had the freedom to make her own choices,
she found her relationships in the home to be deeply
meaningful to her and we could feel her renewed
enthusiasm. To this day we're not really sure what
happened that year but the kids and I discovered that
having a sometimes tired and exhausted "whole person" around the house sure beats living with the dis-
satisfied, demanding lady who used to live there. For
us, Lucy's decision to go back to work helped make our
house a healthier and happier place to be. She had
"come back" and we belonged to each other more than
ever.

The Meaning of Submission

I have included this rather lengthy personal illustration for a purpose. Out of that conflict I began a
thorough reappraisal of my teaching regarding authority and power and the kindred Biblical issues of "submission," "headship," and the so–called "chain of
command." The way in which I had related to my wife
that night was consistent with what I had been taught
and with what I had been teaching others. As a result
of my reappraisal, I have become convinced that my
former understanding of the concepts of submission
and headship had been jaundiced by my male
chauvinism, and that the concept of the "chain of
command" as it is commonly taught is decidedly un-
biblical. Strong words, but nevertheless true.

It's difficult to rethink and undo years of teaching. I

found myself fighting one battle after another. I was forced, I believe by the Spirit of God, to begin at ground zero. The only presupposition I allowed myself was that God's Word is true and that whatever it teaches will be internally consistent. My study of the Scriptures finally sifted the issues down to a few basic passages. My conclusions regarding those Scriptures are as follows:

The first and probably most determinative passage in my search is found in Matthew's Gospel:

> Then the mother of the sons of Zebedee came up to him, with her sons, and kneeling before him she asked him for something. And he said to her, "What do you want?" She said to him, "Command that these two sons of mine may sit, one at your right hand and one at your left, in your kingdom." But Jesus answered, "You do not know what you are asking. Are you able to drink the cup that I am to drink?" They said to him, "We are able." He said to them, "You will drink my cup, but to sit at my right hand and at my left is not mine to grant, but it is for those for whom it has been prepared by my Father." And when the ten heard it, they were indignant at the two brothers.
>
> And Jesus called them to him and said, "You know that the rulers of the Gentiles lord it over them, and their great men exercise authority over them. It shall not be so among you; but whoever would be great among you must be your servant, and whoever would be first among you must be your slave; even as the Son of man came not to be served but to serve, and to give his life as a ransom for many" (Matt. 20:20–28 RSV).

The context of the passage is an occasion when Jesus was alone with his closest followers. At that time the mother of two of his disciples, James and John, approached him and, as is the case of some mothers, began to bargain for a better deal for her boys. She asked that in the kingdom (she thought it would be established in the very near future) her sons be given positions of both prominence and dominance. The import of her request was that they sit on his right and on his left. She wanted them to be Co–Vice Regents, that is, to rule with him. She had probably observed the abilities of the other disciples and had come to the conclusion that her sons were head and shoulders above them all. The reaction of the other disciples was immediate. They became indignant at the two brothers (v. 24). They knew a grab for power when they saw it and they lost no time letting James and John know how they felt.

It is in Jesus' answer that his teaching regarding the issue of power, control, and authority begins to take shape.

In the first place, he tells them that they don't really know what they're asking for. They were anticipating the establishment of an immediate earthly kingdom, and he was anticipating his imminent death. They were looking forward to the glories of being rulers with him, and he was beginning to dread the rigors and humiliation of his trial. Their perceptions of the future involved his domination and judgment of their critics. His perceptions involved the rejection and suffering of the cross.

The disciples and Jesus were looking at the same event from two completely different perspectives. His thinking was "upside–down" to theirs. The "upside–downness" of his thinking can be seen in his evaluation of their perceptions of authority. He challenged their thinking by pointing out that they were patterning themselves not after his teaching but after their pagan oppressors, the Romans.

Authority and Power

"You know that the rulers of the Gentiles lord it over them, and their great men exercise authority over them . . ." (v. 25 RSV). The "rulers of the Gentiles" were the Roman armies who dominated Palestine during the first century. Their rule was often cruel, often unjust, but always consistent in the way authority and power were applied. Who was to be master and who was to be slave was never in doubt. If there were ever a military–political system in which the concept of the "chain of command" was in operation it was in Palestine during Christ's lifetime. Whoever had the "authority" exercised it "over" his subjects.

Parenthetically it's important to note that the way in which authority and power were exercised by the Romans in first century Palestine is exactly the way in which most of us use authority and power today. Those who have the "right to rule," do so by "ruling over." It was the kind of thinking I demonstrated toward my wife in our conflict over her going back to work, and it's the kind of thinking that, in my opinion, controls much of evangelical Christianity. We are preoccupied with who rules whom as much as those in a secular world, a world that functions independently of Christ.

If Jesus wanted to discuss the issues of authority and power, the mother of James and John had provided him with the opportunity. If the Roman concept of the "chain of command" were to characterize their relationships, he could have driven the point home then and there. Instead, he defined for his disciples a way of relating to one another that encompassed a completely "upside–down" way of thinking. He emphasized the role of servant rather than the role of ruler. Verses 26–28 (RSV) demonstrate that he marched to a different drummer: "It shall not be so among you, but whoever would be great among you must be your servant, and whoever would be first among you must be your slave." These verses defined for the disciples that their way of thinking was wrong. It was a position they found impossible to grasp at the time.

The disciples had been seduced into a way of thinking that was concerned with the right and power to rule others rather than concerned with the freedom to serve. They were to be different from the "rulers of the Gentiles."

Part of their "difference" had to do with how far they were to carry their "servanthood." Their example was Jesus himself. The extent to which he was willing to go involved the sacrifice of his own life. In verse 28 we read, "even as the Son of man came not to be served but to serve, and to give his life a ransom for many." His kind of servanthood proved to be a radical departure from the attitudes of the Roman oppressors.

As I studied this verse and its implications for my

own life, I remember asking myself, "Just how far do you go?" It would seem on the surface that you could take this servanthood issue too far. However, I couldn't escape Jesus' example. He was willing to go to the extreme, to the extent of being totally taken advantage of. It was out of his "being taken advantage of" that he demonstrated his obedience to the Father, and out of his obedience came the cross, and out of the cross came the redemption of mankind. If you choose to serve rather than to rule you must be willing to go to the extreme.

My exploration of the servant theme in Scripture didn't end with Matthew 20. Other key passages of Scripture were consistent as well. For example, Jesus' teaching in the upper room as recorded in John 13 is classic. On that occasion, Jesus had, after dinner, wrapped the towel of a slave around his waist and had begun to wash his disciples' feet. One by one they all participated until he came to Peter. Peter's response was in the best tradition of the "chain of command." It didn't make sense that Jesus his Lord should be washing his feet. "Peter said to him, 'Lord, do you wash my feet?' Jesus answered him, 'What I am doing you do not know now, but afterward you will understand.' Peter said to him, 'You shall never wash my feet,' Jesus answered him, 'If I do not wash you, you have no part in me' " (vv. 6–8 RSV). In essence, Peter was insisting that he was to serve Jesus and not vice–versa, but Jesus set him straight. Jesus Christ, the head of the church, was on his knees serving the church, in its earliest form. It is just such an example that the apostle Paul alludes to in Ephesians 5:25: "Husbands, love your wives as Christ also loved the church and gave himself up for her." Rather than insisting on "ruling," husbands are to insist on "serving."

This illustration is critical to the development of the servant theme in Scripture. Jesus had every right in all of God's creation to "rule" the disciples, and Peter, and the church. But there he was on his knees serving rather than "ruling over." His example, his life style, was the exact opposite of a "chain of command."

In terms of the development of the concept of the servanthood of Christ as the pattern we are to follow, the practical application of his example doesn't stop with the disciples, or even with Christian marriage. It is applicable in other relationships as well.

The apostle Peter in his first letter touches on the subject of authority and service in chapter five, verses 1–4. He instructs the elders, or overseers, of the church to "shepherd the flock of God, among you." I like in particular the way in which J. B. Phillips has captured the essence of Peter's instructions:

> Now may I who am myself an elder say a word to you my fellow–elders? I speak as one who actually saw Christ suffer, and as one who will share with you the glories that are to be unfolded. Shepherd your flock of God, looking after them not because you feel compelled to, but willingly, as God would wish. Never do this work thinking of your personal gain but with true compassion. You should aim not at being dictators but examples of Christian living in the eyes of the flock committed to your charge. And then, when the Chief Shepherd reveals himself, you will receive that crown of glory which cannot fade (1 Peter 5:1–4 Phillips).

"Dictators." How apt a description of how authority is so often abused. The relating to others as if they are your mini–fiefdom. How many church squabbles between pastor and people would be avoided if both the congregation and their leaders perceived themselves as servants to one another, on their knees, ready to serve?

This kind of "servant thinking" is found elsewhere in Scripture as well, for example, in the apostle Paul's letter to the Philippians, chapter 2, verses 1–8. To grasp the full meaning of the passage, the context must be explored. In this case Paul was attempting to bridge the gap between two warring factions, each strongly influenced by a woman. In chapter four he writes, "I urge Euodia and I urge Syntyche to live in harmony in the Lord." Who these women were we don't know. We do know, however, that they are called out by name to stop their divisiveness and to work together for the common good of the church. The Philippian church evidently, like many of our churches, was marked by squabbles and disputes. Their witness for the Lord was being affected. They needed to relate to one another differently.

In chapter two of his letter Paul defines exactly how the members of that church were to relate to each other and by application how we as Christians are to relate to one another as well:

> . . . complete my joy by being of the same mind, having the same love, being in full accord and of one mind. Do nothing from selfishness or conceit, but in humility count others better than yourselves. Let each of you look not only to his own interests, but also to the interests of others (Phil. 2:2–4 RSV).

You'll note that they were to work together (verse 2) and they were to defer to one another as the need arose. Paul presupposes that they would by nature look after their own interests but that they needed to be reminded of their responsibility to serve one another (v. 4).

The example they were to follow was the Lord Jesus himself. Verses 5 through 8 form the most clear and explicit explanation of the motivations that lay beneath the sacrifice of Jesus Christ on the cross. He had the right to consider himself to be an equal with the Father (v. 6) and yet he didn't insist on having his own way. Instead, he took the form of a bondslave, the lowest form of servitude, and allowed himself to be abused, humiliated, used, and broken. All without protesting once (Isa. 53:7). How unlike the warring factions of the Philippian church. How much in contrast to the disputings between the races, the sexes, and the nations of our world today. "He humbled himself . . ." and because he humbled himself we can experience the fullness of eternal life.

While it is true that one day he will rule the world with a rod of iron (Phil. 2:9–12), it remains that during this age he chooses to lead by way of example rather than by way of force and coercion.

Another critical passage of Scripture is Paul's letter to the Ephesians, chapters 5 and 6. In looking back upon my earlier impressions regarding the relationship between husbands and wives, this passage is focal.

I can't begin to number the times when I either taught or preached from this passage and always began my messages at verse 22. "Wives, be subject to your husbands, as to the Lord." Oh, how good it felt to begin with those words. I could go on for hours. The only problem was that I was inaccurate in my exegesis of the passage. Paul's thought doesn't begin with verse 22. Unfortunately, not until I committed myself to a thorough restudy of the whole concept of authority did I study the passage in light of its context.

Paul's instruction really begins in verse 15 and ends with a directive that the Ephesian believers be "filled with the Spirit." He was concerned with their Christian walk, and he was concerned with their witness before a pagan world. The practical manifestations or outworkings of what it meant to be filled with the Spirit were threefold, each is expressed in the original Greek by a separate participial phrase. First of all, they were to speak to "one another in Psalms, and hymns and spiritual songs, singing and making melody 'with all their heart' to the Lord." Secondly, they were to give "thanks for all things in the name of our Lord Jesus Christ to God the Father." And, thirdly, they were to be subject, or submissive, "to one another out of reverence for Christ." Being filled with the Spirit involved three manifestations: joyful hearts, thankful attitudes, and *mutually submissive* relationships one to another.

Submission Isn't a One–Way Street

The problem with my earlier interpretations of the passage was that I was forever beginning with the wives submitting and never getting to the place where I talked about husbands submitting to their wives. Submissiveness isn't to be a one–way street.

The apostle was teaching that when wives, husbands, children, fathers or parents, masters and slaves are filled with the Spirit they are *submissive to one another.* When it came to relating to one another, they were to be free to submit or serve the other's needs. Christianity in its earliest forms brought freedom to those who were in bondage. The witness of the early believers in Jesus Christ provided an alternative to the power struggles of the ancient world.

This reemphasis upon the servanthood of Christ as the pattern for our relationships is not without its problems, however. In the first place there is in Scripture the strong teaching that Jesus Christ was the Head of the Church and that the husband, likewise, is to be the head of the wife (1 Cor. 11; Eph. 5). Just exactly what does it mean for the husband to be the "head of the wife"? The traditional interpretation has been that the "head" has the final say, he is the ultimate decision–maker. Frankly, I don't think this squares with Scripture. In the first place, in this age Christ, the Head of the Church, has given us an uncommon degree of freedom in our relationships with him. He has even given mankind the ultimate freedom to reject him. Those who do, of course, will suffer the consequences of their decision, but the fact remains that they still have the freedom to say "no." Whatever "headship" means, it doesn't insist on having its own way.

What it does mean, I think, is that whoever is the

head has the responsibility to lead by way of providing an example, and that the example involves the *greater responsibility to serve*. Admittedly, this is a radical departure from the traditional interpretations of the concept of headship, but I think it follows the example Christ has provided as well as the broader teaching of Scripture.

A second problem concept arises as far as this interpretation of servanthood is concerned. Is the teaching that husbands are to "rule" their wives because of the curse placed upon Eve at the time of the fall (Gen. 3:16)? Again, it is customary to interpret the word "rule" to mean "rule over" in the same way that the Romans ruled the Jews. It is of importance, however, to note that in the Septuagint, the ancient Greek version of the Old Testament, the word that is translated "rule" in Genesis 3:16 is also used by Luke in his gospel account of the same story that Matthew recounted in chapter 20 of his Gospel.

> A dispute also arose among them, which of them was to be regarded as the greatest.
> And he said to them, "The kings of the Gentiles exercise lordship over them; and those in authority over them are called benefactors.
> But not so with you; rather let the greatest among you become as the youngest, and the leader as one who serves" (Luke 22:24–26 RSV).

Jesus radically alters the meaning of the word "rule." He tells his disciples that they are not to "lord it over" one another. Rather, they are to relate to each other in an opposite manner. "Rule" in Genesis 3 must mean something other than "rule over" when it comes to the Christian era.

A helpful parallel passage of Scripture as far as I'm concerned is Paul's instructions to Timothy as found in 1 Timothy 3. In this passage Paul is instructing Timothy as to the qualifications of elders and deacons in the local church. In verses 4, 5, and 12 he says that they are to "manage their own household." The word that is translated "manage" literally means "to stand before," "to lead," or "attend to," indicating caring or a daily maintenance kind of responsibility. The elders were to have given evidence that they were good managers, or "gardeners" of their own families. They were to have given evidence that they were able to shepherd their own families before they were given the responsibility of shepherding the flock of God. In these verses the concept of "rule" does not mean "to rule over." A parallel meaning for "rule" and one that is frequently used in the New Testament is "to be concerned about, to care for, and to give aid to." It is this meaning that squares with Jesus' instructions to his disciples. They were to learn to serve one another in the sense of caring for and bearing one another's burdens. They were not to "lord it over" one another.

Probably nowhere else in Scripture is this better illustrated than in Paul's instructions to husbands as to how they are to treat their wives. He states that husbands are to:

> . . . love their wives as their own bodies. He who loves his wife loves himself. For no man ever hates his own flesh, but nourishes and cherishes it, as Christ does the church (Eph. 5:28, 29 rsv).

A man "rules" his own body in that he takes care of it as a servant does his master. Christ "rules" the church in that he nourishes it and cherishes it. He attends to its needs. When a man assumes the position of "husband," he is, indeed, the head of his wife. He has the greater responsibility to serve and through the example of his service provide leadership, not only to his wife but also to his family.

I have come to realize that this interpretation of "headship" is extremely threatening, especially to those of us who have operated in the traditional role of husband, those of us who insist upon having the final say in everything. I remember talking with an irate husband following one of my speaking engagements. With eyes raging he confronted me with the supposed fact that if he were to go to such extremes, his wife would take advantage of him and the full weight (or work) of the family would fall on his shoulders. I tried to sympathize with his fear (he refused to label it that) and to encourage him to try being a servant to his wife just once. He, of course, said that he had tried and that it hadn't worked. I asked how long he had tried and he replied, "One week." I suggested that it probably would take longer than one week, but unfortunately my argument didn't budge him a bit. The last time I saw him he had spun on his heals muttering under his breath that I was some kind of "fuzzy–headed feminist" and that he longed for the good old days when people just taught the Bible instead of psychology.

My usual response to his kind of criticism, I admit, has been mixed. At first I would become defensive, wanting to overcome all objections with the weight of my arguments. But I have since come to realize that the concept of servanthood with all of its paradox is as difficult to grasp today as it was in the time of Christ. How I respond to criticism can take the form of insisting on my own way, another form of "lording it over" another, or I can see myself as my critic's servant, leaving the rightness or wrongness of my position to be tested by time and to be vindicated or rejected by the Holy Spirit.

The application for today is obvious. This issue of who serves whom is to be of controlling interest to the Christian rather than who rules whom. But how often and how easily do we forget? Husbands and wives, males and females, parents and teenagers, blacks and whites, citizens and governments, all too easily become preoccupied with the pursuit of power, or the right to rule.

It seems to me that the church must once again exert the example of its own service. In so doing it will regain the opportunity to provide an alternative mode of relationship, the privilege of emulating Jesus Christ.

I close with an extended but highly relevant quote from Mark Hatfield, the United States Senator from Oregon. His words are an excellent summary of what this chapter is all about.

> Service to others, solely for their own behalf and even entailing deep sacrifice, is the true essence of leadership and the ultimate form of power. There is a power in servanthood which transcends all notions of power

sought after so avidly in the secular political sphere of life.

All this is evidenced most clearly in the person of Jesus of Nazareth. Regardless of one's own personal religious beliefs, anyone would have to conclude that this man exercised a form of power which changed totally the course of history. Yet what was the nature of that power? What was the style of his leadership? It was a form of seeming powerlessness, expressed in self-sacrificial love and service on the behalf of others. His leadership was the surrendering of his personal prerogatives, the giving up of his ego; it was just the opposite of what the world estimates true leadership to be. His power consisted solely in his radical faithfulness to a vision. He called this vision the "Kingdom of God," and he defined this calling as "doing his Father's will." His method for accomplishing these ends was not to seek public acclaim or devise a calculated strategy, but rather to surrender in utter faithfulness to God's will, exemplifying through a total self-giving love the heart and the message of his mission.*

Only when we are free to serve others are we "free indeed."

*Mark Hatfield, *Between a Rock and a Hard Place* (Waco: Word, 1976), pp. 26–27.

3

Free to Fail

Free to Fail

There was a time when life was basic and simple. The issues of life had to do with the matter of existence, whether or not you had enough to eat, a place for your family to sleep and stay warm. For most Christians in the Western world those issues are settled. We have shelter and food. In their place we have substituted other issues, more complex in nature. We have become preoccupied not with the maintenance of life but with the quality of life. Most of us don't worry about having enough to eat, but whether we will have fresh or frozen vegetables. We are preoccupied not with shelter for the night but with the relative size of our homes, how many bedrooms we have compared with the neighbors down the street. We are an affluent people caught in a treadmill that insists that life must always be getting bigger and better.

There is a fallout that results from our preoccupation with the quality of life. This fallout covers both Christian and non–Christian alike. It flows naturally out of a system of priorities that emphasizes the "bigger" and the "better." The fallout is our preoccupation with success and the dread of failure. The irony of it all is that the emphasis upon success brings about its own defeat. No one can always be successful no matter how competent he is. Failure at some time in life and in one form or another is inevitable. Yet we live our lives as if failure is to be avoided at all costs. We are caught in the bind between the need to succeed and the likelihood of failure. The result is unfortunate. Many who experience failure, even for the first time, come to see themselves as failures, losers in the game of life.

The pressure to succeed and the fear of failure in some ways is the benchmark of our society. We glamorize those in public view, pay them inflated salaries, and dream that we might one day be like them. And the church, the body of Christ, is sucked into the same trap. We, like the world, make heroes of those who are successful and venerate them as models to copy, ideals to emulate.

Although the church defines success differently than does the world, the fact remains that we are forever impressed with those who have "made it big." Success for us is the individual who has won hundreds or thousands to Christ, the pastor of a large and growing church whose Sunday school numbers in the thousands, the professional athlete who has turned to Christ. The list goes on and on, characterized by a common thread. We are impressed with the "bigger" and the "better." We are impressed with success.

What about those of us who are just ordinary people struggling in our Christian lives? What happens to us when we let "success" be defined for us in ways we will never be able to achieve? What about those of us who will never see ourselves as "successful" as the church defines it? The results are inevitable. We come to see ourselves as failures, as losers.

My Own Experience

An especially vivid experience in my own journey as a Christian illustrates the issue. On one occasion a popular, dynamic Christian leader had come to our school to discuss those issues in the Christian life particularly of interest to him. In his case, he was deeply committed to personal evangelism. We had been stirred by his chapel message and had been challenged to reevaluate our responsibilities as evangelists. I had walked out of the chapel personally convicted that I ought to be doing more. When I walked out I was excited as well because I had been asked by one of the faculty to drive our guest back to his hotel. The speaker was one of my heroes. I had observed him from a distance for a period of years and had been indirectly touched by his ministry. There was much about him that I wished were a part of me. He didn't know it but I was impressed just sitting in the same car with him.

As we neared his hotel he asked if I had time to let him run up to his hotel room and then take him to his next appointment? I had more than enough time. We parked the car on the street and walked toward the hotel. I was impressed. As busy as he was and as famous as he was, he was still interested in me. I felt a little "puppylike" as we talked, and I found myself hoping he wouldn't notice how nervous I was.

After walking through the lobby of the hotel we came to the elevator. My "hero" greeted the operator by his first name (again I was impressed), and we began the ten–story trip to the top. To my complete amazement my leader/model began to share his faith with the elevator operator and to my complete surprise after a short conversation in the tenth floor hall the operator bowed his head and prayed to receive Christ. I had witnessed a miracle and it had taken less than ninety seconds. I couldn't believe it. We said good-by to our new Christian brother and walked to the leader's room. It was obvious that what had happened was a simple fact of his life. It happened every day. In his room he placed a call to confirm his next appointment.

Unfortunately, the appointment had to be rescheduled and he decided that he would stay in his room and rest until it was time for him to go. I caught the hint and excused myself. As I walked toward the elevator I decided to try my hand at elevator evangelism. I punched the button and waited for the elevator to come. A hurried prayer preceded my entrance and we began our journey downward. As I had seen it done just ten minutes before in the elevator to our right I broached the subject of Christ using the same words with, I would imagine, the same voice inflection. I "shared" Christ and accomplished my task with three or four seconds to spare as the door opened for the main floor. I anxiously waited for the elevator operator's reply.

"What! You must be out of your mind, kid. Get out of here before I call the manager and he throws you out."

I was completely and totally rebuffed. As I walked out of the hotel and toward my car I gave myself the usual pep talk about some "sowing" and some "watering" and some "reaping." But try as I might I couldn't shake the feeling that somehow I had failed. I was a defeated Christian and felt that if I had only been "Spirit–filled" the result would have been different. Without realizing it, that event affected my evangelistic zeal for years to come.

I have since taken the occasion to reflect upon that experience and to assess its impact upon my life. Whether it makes sense to anyone else or not, the fact remains that I walked away from the event in my life convinced that something was wrong with me and that if I worked hard enough I could become just like my hero. I have since changed my mind.

What, Really, Is Success?

In the first place, I had fallen into the trap of defining success for me in terms of what was success for him. I had come to believe that somehow everything he could do I could do, too. It was as if I were a little leaguer just learning to swing the bat and I had chosen a champion major–leaguer as my idol. I wouldn't be successful until I could hit, run, and throw like he could. The gauge in my own mind as to what constituted "success" made it something that was beyond me, at least at that point in my life. My definition of success cancelled out any difference due to spiritual gift, experience, and Christian maturity. I couldn't do what he had done and the feeling that swept over me was one of failure.

The situations that parallel mine are legion. For example, I recently talked with a middle–aged pastor who had just finished his twentieth year of ministry. He was emotionally depressed to the point of walking away from his ministry. When we talked at length about his feelings, I realized that he, like me, had been caught with his thermometer showing. He had been taking his spiritual and emotional temperature, using others as his measurement of success. A dynamic young pastor had moved into his area and his presence had turned the Christian community upside down. The young pastor's church had more than quadrupled in membership in less than three years. His sanctuary was being tripled in size and the Christians were flocking to his church like lemmings to the sea. And to top it all off, his church had begun a "tape ministry" and was supplying thousands of believers all over the world with tapes of his sermons.

Needless to say some of those tapes had found their way into the homes and cars of the troubled pastor's parishioners. Every time he preached he found himself comparing his message with the style and delivery of the "successful" pastor. Whenever a family in his church moved its membership to the "successful" church he felt himself to be a dismal failure. No amount of reassurance was able to help him feel differently. "Success" had come to be defined as a tape ministry, a big sanctuary, a large Sunday school, and so on. He had none of those and as a result he saw himself as a "loser," a failure.

If he were your pastor what would you say to him?

Even better, if he were your husband what would be your response? I'm sure most of us would try to encourage him in one of two ways. Either we would draw attention to what we thought were his "successes," or we would downplay the "successes" of the young pastor with whom he was comparing himself.

"He may be a good preacher, but nobody cares for their flock like you do." Or, "Numbers aren't really important, it's quality that counts." Or even further, "Don't compare yourself with him. If you look at the churches in our denomination, we've grown more than 65 percent of them during the last three years. Not everybody is meant to be Baptists (or Independents, or Methodists, or Presbyterians, and so on)."

The tendency is to play the same game but to change the rules to help your side win. What I would suggest as an alternative is more radical than changing the rules. It has to do with questioning whether or not we should be in the "success game" at all. By this I mean that the "success/failure" dilemma we find ourselves in is doomed from the beginning because its basic rationale is characteristic of the world rather than the kingdom of God. The change I am suggesting would involve more than just a change in the rules, it would involve a change in our thinking.

I'm convinced that failure is devastating to most of us because we have come to believe that approval, whether it is the approval of self, others, or God, is dependent upon how we perform. Failure to perform, and the flip–side of the problem, the fear of the failure to perform, haunts us like the ghosts of Christmas past.

If I am to change my thinking about this, I must deliberately focus upon the "here and now" and the richness of the moment rather than upon the end result.

My dialogue with the veteran, troubled pastor illustrates what I mean.

"What happened in your ministry this week?"

"Nothing."

"Were you in bed all week?"

"No."

"Then what happened?"

"I just prepared for my Sunday sermons like I usually do, made a few calls, and spent the rest of the week being depressed. Sounds kind of self-piteous, doesn't it?"

"That's irrelevant to me at this point. Whom did you call on?"

"A young couple who had visited the church and a little gray-haired old lady who's dying of cancer. Nothing spectacular."

"Nothing spectacular is your judgment upon yourself and we've pretty well established that you're not the most objective critic at this point in your ministry. Let's look at your calls and see whether or not 'nothing happened.' "

"Well, the couple was having marital problems, but it was more than I could handle so I referred them to a Christian psychologist in the area."

"Was that a victory or a defeat using your thermometer of success?"

"I don't know. I hadn't really thought about it. I

guess it was a success, but, if I'm honest, it feels like a defeat."

"Have you done any follow–up?"

"Yes. They've been back to church and they're going for counseling."

"But you don't see that as a success, do you?"

"No. I guess I don't."

"I think your thinking is all messed up. God touched the lives of a young couple through you, but you weren't able to enjoy the privilege of being used because you've distorted what success is all about. What about the little old lady?"

"Well. We talked about death, we talked about her relationship to Christ, and I prayed with her. And that was it."

"Had anyone else talked to her about dying?"

"No. I was the first. Once we got on the subject she talked for over an hour. I guess she was lonely."

"Maybe nobody had talked with her about death. That happens a lot, you know."

"I hadn't really thought that much about it."

He "hadn't thought that much about it." His response was typical. God had used him to touch the lives of three hurting, isolated, and lonely people during the week, but his mind was elsewhere. He was worried about his sermon and he was worried about his pastoral performance as measured by the "bigger" and the "better."

I found my heart aching for him. He was truly a gentle and godly man, a servant of God with whom Jesus is well pleased. But he's not able to bask in the warmth of God's pleasure. He sees only the disapproval of his critics and he is his own worst critic. He had backed himself into a corner through his preoccupation with success. The sad fact is that preoccupation with success usually deemphasizes people and in their place substitutes numbers, or programs, or organizations. Things win over people. When that happens I'm sure God is not pleased.

People Are More Important Than Things

Making people to be more important than things is the first step in redefining our thinking about success and failure. It is the difference between being a housewife and a homemaker, a preacher and a pastor, a machine and a man. The world dehumanizes people but kingdom thinking restores their importance.

There is a second issue that needs to be settled if we are to become free with respect to our attitude toward failure. It has to do with a deemphasis upon heroes. In a sense it's another way of looking at the issue I've just discussed, that of placing an emphasis upon people rather than things.

What makes a man or a woman a hero? When you evaluate what makes someone a hero it's usually in terms of something he's done or some talent or ability he has, the expression of which involves power, money, or some physical characteristic. Sports figures, entertainers, politicians, captains of industry, all derive their status through the accumulation or manipulation of things. Seldom are the people who are good with people deemed to be heroes. The teachers, the mothers and fathers, the youth leaders, the "people–people" are rarely given a position of prominence in today's world.

Unfortunately, in my opinion, the Christian community has been caught in the same snare. Who are the heroes of the Christian world? The authors, the speakers, the leaders of organizations, all are attributed the status of superstars without a thought of the implications as to what that means.

What impresses me about kingdom thinking is the presence of "upside–down thinking." Jesus said that the least shall be the greatest, the last shall be first, he who would live must first die. His kind of thinking just doesn't make sense in the world today. The same upside–down kind of thinking holds true when it comes to heroes in the kingdom of God. The least, the last, the smallest and the servants are the greatest in God's sight. I would imagine that many of us who see ourselves as failures when judged by the criteria of today's world may well be "heroes" according to the criteria of the kingdom. But because we have been conformed to the world in our thinking we just can't see it.

Henry David Thoreau, the American poet, has put it well: "Why should we be in such desperate haste to succeed, and in such desperate enterprises? If a man does not keep pace with his companions, perhaps it is because he hears a different drummer. Let him step to the music which he hears, however measured or far away."

When it comes to the kingdom of God, he is a hero who will hear, "Well done, thou good and faithful servant. Enter into thy rest."

Seeing Life As a Whole

There is a third and last dimension to my analysis of failure that I believe is relevant. It has to do with what I have come to see as our preoccupation with the part rather than the whole. By this I mean that a single event or even a series of events do not constitute the whole of a man's or woman's life. Mistakes are often the preamble to growth, especially when it comes to the Christian life. Following the apostle Paul's reasoning in Romans 5, tribulations (in the case of many of us, the "failures") bring about perseverance, perseverance proves our character, and character brings hope. Hope makes us aware of the love of God that has been shed abroad in our lives. Most of us, it would seem to me, want to experience the fullness of the love of God without the necessary preamble of tribulation.

If John Mark, who had been sent packing by the apostle Paul because of his "failure" (Acts 15:38), had reacted as many of us react, the kingdom would have been robbed of one of its staunchest early defenders. The same holds true of the apostle Peter. If there ever was a failure it was Peter. He was a braggart and he was boastful. He said he would never deny the Lord. And yet, his denial was the most visible and in some ways the most blatant. The searing pain of his failure remained with him long after his restoration by the Lord.

It is of interest to me that when Jesus confronted Peter after his denial (John 21:15–17), the confrontation did not involve Peter's performance. It did involve Peter's commitment. Jesus drew Peter's attention to the relationship between the two of them and not to the tasks that Peter should have accomplished.

I think that the same holds true for us. What is at stake when we fail is not the issue of our performance. The issue is how that "failure" affects our relationship to Jesus and our relationships to others. Peter's failure had an immeasurable impact upon his entire ministry for his Lord. He was never the same again. God used that series of events to humble and equip him for future service. At the moment it happened it seemed to be a devastating loss. But in the context of Peter's entire life it was a necessary chapter, the seed-bed for growth.

Recently I had occasion to prepare a series of messages from Paul's letter to the Romans, chapter 8. At the same time in my counseling practice many of my patients seemed to be afflicted with the despair and disillusionment of failure. Nervous breakdowns, divorces, rebellious teen-agers—everyone was plagued with the reality of his own loss and pain. My response was to unconsciously take on their despair as my own. Together we struggled, and together we failed.

Frankly, out of knee–jerk habit I had encouraged some of them to seek solace in the Word of God. But I had not heeded my own counsel. My heart was heavy and my inability to "heal" them weighted me down intolerably. Quite by accident I found myself in Romans 8. The text was verses 33 through 39, especially verse 35: "Who shall separate us from the love of Christ? shall tribulation, or distress, or persecution, or famine, or nakedness, or peril, or sword?" As I studied Paul's words more closely I came to see that most of the phenomena he listed were, in fact, the same phenomena my patients were struggling with.

"Tribulation"—the pressure of a burdened spirit, in other words, depression.

"Distress"—the anguish of the inner soul, or anxiety.

"Persecution"—the chronic or nagging problems of everyday life.

"Famine"—physical hunger to the point of death.

"Nakedness"—to be poorly clothed, unemployed, chronically poor.

"Peril"—emotional danger, fears, the threat of rejection.

"Sword"—physical danger, the threat of the loss of life through accident or aggression.

The list was incredibly similar to the list of pains and hurts being suffered by my patients. Paul's declaration was that none of these events can separate us from the love of Christ. But, unfortunately, there was one thing missing. Some of my patients at that time were not concerned about the love of Christ. More concerned with the immediacy of their situation, they were finding it difficult to see beyond the struggles in the here and now. There had to be an answer.

The answer was in the next verse: "For thy sake we are killed all the day long." The words "for thy sake . . ." kept tumbling over and over in my mind. They formed at least a beginning answer to the dilemma faced by my patients. If they could see that whatever intrudes into their lives can be used by God in some way for his glory then nothing is meaningless and useless. The greater issue is whether the individual Christian is willing or not to surrender himself or herself to Christ. When Christ is Lord and we are his servants, even the failures of life, the tribulations, the distresses, the perils, and so on, have meaning. Christ's promise is not to turn the pain into pleasure, or the anguish into joy. His promise is that whatever happens to us, no matter how severe, we can yield that experience to him to be used for his glory and he promises that we will experience the love in the midst.

Since that time I have tried to help my patients see the broader purpose for their "failures." In the first place, many times they are measuring themselves using the thermometers of the contemporary world rather than the measurements of the kingdom of God. God's definition of success and our definition are usually dramatically different. Only when we begin to align our perspectives with his do we begin to see life and our experiences as he sees them, and our preoccupation with success is rendered meaningless.

Second, and corollary to the first, is our preoccupation with heroes. We seem to evidence a need to identify with the "best" in contemporary society. Unfortunately, the "best" in today's world is often the worst according to the "upside–down" thinking of the kingdom of God. If left to itself, the world will inevitably choose those who are the farthest from the kingdom of God rather than the closest. The impact upon me, if I am experiencing failure or see myself as a failure, is to ask myself whom have I chosen to be my "heroes"? My choices are a clear–cut indication of my value system and it is my value system that provides the criteria by which I measure success or failure. It is impossible to select heroes who are antithetical to the kingdom of God without the values behind that selection becoming dominant in life. It is a curious phenomenon that when you begin to redefine your value system according to what you see to be values consistent with kingdom thinking, much of what is defined as "failure" takes on a different hue. Its impact is not nearly as great.

Last of all, becoming "free to fail" involves the belief that what is happening to me today cannot be interpreted apart from the whole of my life. The tendency is to see our lives as a series of parentheses with each event being experienced separately from the others. That needn't be so. When seen from God's perspective, the events of our lives are not distinct parentheses but individual threads in a tapestry. The greater issue is God's purpose for weaving that tapestry. Do the inner weavings of my life belong to me or to him? When I bring my life to him, even with its failures, I experience his love, and then, and only then, am I "free to fail."

4

Free to Be Angry

Free to Be Angry

"David! Come in this house this very minute." Just seconds before, David, a three–year–old, tow–headed little boy had defended his honor and had pushed the little girl from down the street, and she had fallen backward over her tricycle. She had refused to move when he had roared up on his brand new Big Wheel. Screaming as if she had been mortally wounded, she had raced home to inform her mother how viciously she had been attacked. A clash of wills and the sparks of anger had resulted in a neighborhood trauma. What should the mothers do?

David's mother grabbed him by the arm as he came in the front door and marched him down the hall to his room.

"David, I'm ashamed of you. Don't you know that little boys shouldn't hit little girls? And besides, I'm sure that if Jesus were here right now, he would be very upset with you. God doesn't like his children to be angry."

And so a Christian mother asserted the unspoken dogma of centuries: God gets angry with angry people.

Down the street the other mother was dealing with the same problem.

"Hit him back. Crying and running home isn't going to help. Little girls must learn to take care of themselves. You can't expect someone else to fight your battles for you. The next time he pushes you down, get right back up and hit him in the face. He'll probably think twice before he does it again."

This mother added a new twist to an old teaching. "Little girls, like little boys, can operate under the rules of an eye for an eye and a tooth for a tooth." Two extremes, yet typical of how the mothers of this generation are handling their children's conflicts.

How to Handle Anger

Which mother was right? How should they instruct their children in the management of their anger? The first mother has the tradition of the church behind her and the second has the momentum of contemporary thinking behind her. How each resolves the problem will deeply program into her child's unconscious how he/she should manage his anger as an adult. The long–term implications of the event are far–reaching, extending years ahead to the child's adult life.

Each of us in fact has had similar messages programed into our unconscious. Each has learned a repertoire of responses whenever we experience the emotion we call anger. We have received David's "mother-like" messages, or we have received messages fitted to the spirit of the times. All of us, without exception, have learned a strategy for managing our anger, and each strategy is either working effectively for us or it isn't. I am especially concerned with those strategies that don't work. It is my observation that in the Christian community the strategies we most often use work the least effectively of all. Something must be wrong.

It's my firm conviction that we, as Christians, have perverted the New Testament teachings regarding what I believe to be a normal, God–given human emotion, the emotion of anger. We have had programed into us and into our children not the teachings of Scripture but the teachings of our traditions. We are sincere and we are earnest, but we are wrong. Years later our children reap the consequences of our error as we are reaping the consequences of errors of our parents, and they of their parents. My purpose in this chapter is to examine the various strategies for handling anger, most of which don't work, and to seek to establish an alternative strategy, one based upon the teaching of Scripture. One that, hopefully, works.

The Ways We Handle Anger

My suggestions on establishing a biblical strategy for handling anger will be threefold. In the first place I would like to examine the ways most of us handle anger, ways that usually don't work. Secondly, I'd like to attempt to legitimatize the God–given character of the emotion of anger. And thirdly, I'd like to outline a methodology for processing anger constructively rather than destructively. I realize the task is formidable, but it is necessary if we as Christians are to begin to deal effectively with our emotions. When we do, we will begin to experience what it means to be "free indeed."

There are hundreds of ways to catalog the dysfunctional means of processing anger. The short space of the chapter before us does not allow for a full evaluation and discussion of the issue. In fact, whole psychological theories have been forged based solely on learning how to express the emotion of anger. But in the limited space before us, I'll at least attempt to broach the issue. I have found it personally helpful to classify the mishandling of anger into five cagetories.

The "Stamp Saver"

The "stamp saver" is the first culprit in the mishandling of anger. I'm sure that most of us at one time or another have been given trading stamps. When we would go to the market or to the gas station, the merchant would give us trading stamps for shopping at his establishment. Later, usually months later for most of us, we would gather up all the trading stamps in the house and spend the better part of an evening licking them and then pasting them into a book. When we had enough books, we would bunch them together and hurry down to the Blue Chip or Green Stamp store. There on the shelves before us would be the premiums ripe for the trading.

If we had been exceptionally frugal and conscientious we would spread scores of stamp books onto the counter and the clerk would obediently retrieve the gift or gifts we had chosen. At the appropriate time we would redeem our stamps for the desired goods. This analogy of trading stamps has been used by a psychiatrist named Eric Berne to describe what many of us do with our anger. We save it up in bits and pieces until we have accumulated a sufficient amount and then we "trade" our angers in, usually to the complete confusion of the recipient.

I don't like to admit it but I'm a stamp–saver. I remember on one Saturday morning I had decided to sleep in. My visions the night before were that, come morning, I would peacefully doze, occasionally waking, only to go back to sleep, all of the time enjoying the absolute luxury of my bed. However, my fantasies were short lived. Crisply at seven o'clock in the morning, Shannon, our youngest daughter, awakened with her usual early morning gusto. She has the ability to instantly roll out of bed with all of her faculties working and to be off and about her day, moving at full tilt the minute the covers are thrown back. On that particular morning she had chosen as her first item of business to play one of her children's records. Cheerfully she placed the first record on the turntable and gently from her room came the sounds of Marcy, the children's puppet. Now this, I'm sure, sounds quite harmless. It was, except for the fact that Shannon's room is immediately adjacent to ours and that her record player was butted up against our common wall. Before Marcy had sung the first line of the first verse I was awake and I was angry.

"Shannon! For crying out loud, turn that record player off. Don't you know that there are some of us in this house still trying to sleep!" My pious "righteous indignation" snaked around the corner from our room to hers and shook her.

Now Shannon knows better than to test me at those times. I'm sure that she's learned when a certain volume and tone are combined in my voice, irrespective of what I'm saying, it's time to snap to and do what she's told. So, obediently, she lifted the arm off the record and proceeded on with her morning. But what should she do and where should she go? As is her custom, she migrated to the family room where the television and its Saturday morning children's cartoons beckoned seductively.

After what seemed to me to be a few short moments (if the truth were known it was probably a half hour or more), the sounds of the Roadrunner with his infernal "beep-beep" came streaking down the hall from the family room to our bedroom.

This time the irritation in my voice was unmistakable. "Shannon! Didn't you hear what I said? Turn off the television before I come out there and give you a spanking!"

The sounds from the family room went completely silent, only it was too late. My Saturday morning fantasy had been sabotaged by the combined efforts of the record industry and the television networks all craftily orchestrated by the cunning mind of my five–year–old child. The war was on, or at least it must have seemed so from Shannon's point of view. Throughout the day she did things that irritated me terribly, all without her realizing what she was doing. After each irritation I glued one of those anger stamps into the book I was keeping in my mind.

The bookkeeping process wasn't complicated. It had become so routine as to become unconscious through the years. I was in the habit of accumulating my angry feelings inside, rarely acknowledging to others at the time that I was angry. Later I would let it all hang out, usually at a time that was to my advantage. Then I would label it "righteous indignation" rather than anger. That way I would never have to apologize for my anger or appear to be unspiritual.

Later that evening at dinner I decided to trade in my stamps. Poor Shannon, she didn't know it was coming. The opportunity presented itself when she accidentally spilled her milk having been warned not to do so earlier in the meal.

"What in the world is wrong with you?" I raged. "Can't you do anything right? Sometimes it looks like you're just trying to get into trouble." On and on I went, hammering away with my indignation. The poor kid. She began to sob.

"Daddy, I just spilled my milk."

But I wouldn't let her off the hook. I had a whole day's worth of anger stored up and she had to pay the consequences. The only problem was, and so it is with the victims of stamp–savers, my anger was out of proportion to the event that precipitated it. Why get so excited over a glass of spilled milk? To a child who begins with the assumption that his parent is always right and he is always wrong, the only conclusion he can draw is that there must be something dreadfully wrong with him, else why would daddy or mommy be so angry? Shannon's acceptance of being such a "bad person" was more than I could take. Frankly, I don't remember how long it took before I was able to admit to God, to myself, and most of all to Shannon that I was wrong, but I know eventually I did. The only problem is that I still, to this day, have to watch myself to keep me from doing the same thing. Just knowing you're a stamp–saver doesn't keep you from being a stamp–saver. Whatever the cause, its effects are extremely hard on others and it certainly falls into the category of "mishandled anger."

"Scapegoating"

The second way of mishandling anger in my classification system is "scapegoating." The historical antecedent for this process is found in the Old Testament.

> And when he has made an end of atoning for the holy place and the tent of meeting and the altar, he shall present the live goat; and Aaron shall lay both his hands upon the head of the live goat, and confess over him all the iniquities of the people of Israel, and all their transgressions, and their sins; and he shall put them upon the head of the goat, and send him away into the wilderness by the hand of a man who is in readiness. The goat shall bear all their iniquities upon him to a solitary land; and he shall let the goat go in the wilderness (Lev. 16:20–22 RSV).

The goat bears the iniquities of the people. In the case of scapegoating and anger, the average scenerio would go something like this. Mom is irritated at dad because he hasn't cleaned the garage as he promised. Weekend after weekend has passed and a whole year's worth of junk has accumulated. She's hinted, she's asked, she's begged, and she's seduced but to no avail. Her bag of womanly tricks is depleted. As a "total" or "fascinating" woman she's a flop. What remains is anger, not the kind of anger that passes easily, but the kind of anger that seethes down deep inside, and makes each instance of his neglect feel like he doesn't really care. "If he really loved me he wouldn't treat me this way."

There is a deeper problem, however. Deep inside she's really afraid of her husband, afraid that if she's not good to him he'll do something drastic, like leave her. The threat is always present although they've never talked about it, and it may in fact, have never crossed his mind. It is, unfortunately, part of the mortar that holds her emotions toward him in check. What does she do with her anger? Put it on someone else, of course.

On this Saturday afternoon she elbows her way through the disheveled garage and into the kitchen. The garage's disarray is total. Every conceivable inch of space has been given over to piles and piles of junk. She's furious but she can't tell her husband lest she interrupt his college football game on television. Aimlessly she wanders down the hall toward the bedrooms. Quite by accident, she walks by the half–open, or perhaps the half–concealed, bedroom door of her teen–age daughter. She reaches out and pushes the door full open. What she sees is the garage in miniature. Instead of the car there is the bed. Strung throughout the room are piles of clothes, unwashed gym suits, the Sunday funnies for the past three weeks, record albums, shredded Elton John wall posters, empty lipsticks, and so on. The sight is more than she can handle. With the shriek of a charging Apache she bellows her daughter's name. The kid, unknowingly, peers around the corner at the end of the hall.

"Get down here and clean up this pig–pen! What's wrong with you? I'd be ashamed to live in such a mess if I were you!" The verbal assault spreads like an oil spill until the daughter begins to feel as if it will never stop and she'll be smothered by her mother's rage. Finally, after sufficient ventilation, the mother's anger subsides until another day when she'll storm and rage at some other unsuspecting soul. In the meantime her teen–aged daughter will, herself, have learned to seethe inside, like her mother, and soon will begin to drain off her anger on unsuspecting others as well.

Scapegoating is obviously destructive. The dreadful result of this way of processing anger is that it's usually the weak and the young who are selected as the "scapegoat." They are forced to bear the sins of others without having the privilege of even enjoying the sin itself. They learn either to perceive themselves as hopeless martyrs or to vent their own ire on others as it has been vented on them. The process is passed from generation to generation like a hereditary malformity that distorts even the healthiest of relationships. It is passed on until someone interrupts the process and becomes "free" to behave otherwise.

Depression

The third way we often mishandle anger is one of the most common of all. We normally refer to it as "depression." When I talk about this kind of depression, I'm referring to something more than the usual "blue Mondays," or even "down" days. It's more than the "blahs." What I'm referring to is a kind of inward blackness that sucks at one's insides and eats away any and all vestiges of hope and joy. This kind of depression is the sort that can end with a suicide attempt, chronic alcoholism, or even acute psychosis. It feels to the sufferer to be more than he can possibly handle.

Where does this kind of depression come from? When one of my patients begins to describe his symptoms and I sense that he is suffering from this terrible pain, I often ask, "Whom do you think you're mad at?" The patient is usually startled by the question and his first response is typically, "No one." He begins describing the symptoms over again to me as if I hadn't heard the first time and ends only when I question him a second time.

"I'm sorry. I guess I didn't clearly express myself. I meant to ask, 'Whom do you hate?' " By this time the patient is irritated. "I didn't say that I hate anyone. All I said was that I was depressed."

"I'm sorry," I reply, "I think it's important that from the beginning you understand that I believe most often the roots of depression, the kind you've described to me, are really unresolved angers, angers that have been accumulated to the point of hatred." Typically the patient shakes his head in disbelief and slumps back into his chair, too tired to protest yet desperate that something be done. It takes four to six counseling sessions, on the average, before he is able to admit that he's mad at someone even if it is himself.

Depression of this kind is usually anger turned inward. It is the accumulated result of hundreds, even thousands, of angers that have been swallowed to the point they've lodged in the inward soul of the person as barnacles lodge on the hull of a ship. Soon the ship begins to slow, to wallow in the seas with the weight of its below–the–surface cargo. The ship stops, near panic ensues, with the crew unsure and unsteady.

Christians who have been told as little children that "God gets angry at angry little boys and girls" often grow up and find themselves to be victims of depression, convinced that something is wrong with their "seamanship." If only they were better able to "navigate life" they wouldn't be depressed. My response to that kind of thinking is "rubbish."

It's not that we're poor navigators, it's that we've been taught to mishandle a very common emotion and the end result is worse than what we repressed in the first place.

It's important to note who we, as Christians, are most often angry at. On the surface we are usually angry at ourselves or someone in our immediate family, such as a husband or a wife. The next level the anger can be found is with a divorced or deceased spouse. The depressed person feels himself or herself to have been capriciously left alone and deserted, and the result is depression. The third and most common focus of repressed anger is often one or both parents. Most often we have been genuinely mishandled or mistreated by our parents in such a way as to cause deep hurt. The problem, however, is that we've never been given permission to be angry at our parents, even symbolically. We have been "provoked to wrath" (Eph. 6:4) but have learned to deny that we are angry and instead we push it inside where it festers for years, only to surface at a later date.

The last, and perhaps the least likely candidate for our anger, is God himself. I'm surprised how many Christians are really very angry at God but have never been able to be honest with him about it. The fact remains that in any relationship, even one with God, anger is a normal and natural by–product. Is it ever right and proper to get mad at God? Doesn't that mean you're out of fellowship? Not necessarily. In fact, I've found in my own experience that getting mad at God and letting him know truthfully how I felt was the only way I was going to be able to maintain communication with him.

It all happened a day or two after our four–and–a–half–year–old son had died. My grief was more than I could bear and I found myself asking God why he hadn't kept Stevie from falling into that swimming pool. If he were God, why didn't he take care of my little boy? I soon realized that my questions were really accusations. I was only playing games with God. If I were to go on serving him I needed to let him know exactly how I felt. But how do you do that and where do you go to do it? My solution was to go for a ride on the freeway with the windows of my car rolled up. As the car gathered speed so did my emotions. Soon I was yelling at God with all the rage that was within me. I even called him some names that I thought I had forgotten, names that were part of the streets of my boyhood years.

I remember yelling, then sobbing, then apologizing, and then asking for forgiveness for anything I had said that was wrong or inappropriate. But I also remember another impression at the time. God could handle it. He wasn't about to turn tail and desert me now. God doesn't get angry at angry people. Quite the contrary. He understands them because he helped manufacture the system that includes their emotions. God could handle my anger. He wouldn't go away.

Many times in the quiet and protective surroundings of my office I have encouraged my patients to go ahead and be honest about their anger with God. It's not that they're not angry, it's only that they've not been honest about it. Many times believing God to have moved away from them because of their anger, they begin to move away from him. The distance, the alienation, grows each day the anger is allowed to go unprocessed. I usually encourage them to have a conversation, out loud, with God in which they tell him exactly how they feel, not pulling any punches. I'm sure some of you as you read this will conclude that this is blasphemy. My own experience and observation is exactly the opposite. The blasphemy more often comes because of the denial not because of the truth. It is possible to love someone and be angry at him at the same time—even God. Only children think this isn't so. When it comes to God, to pretend you have no anger toward him when, in fact, you do, and that you feel only love, is the surest way to eventually kill your love. If you are angry at God, admit it. Go ahead and be honest with him. He can handle it.

Psychosomatic Illness

The next way of mishandling anger to be discussed in this chapter is what physicians have come to label, "psychosomatic illness." It is illness that is real in the sense that it is not imagined, but it is illness that is psychologically based. Some illnesses are brought about because of disease, or because of the malfunction of some physical organ. There are, however, times when a patient becomes ill but the basic cause for the illness lies not with disease or biological malfunction. It is an illness that originates in or is aggravated by the emotional processes of the individual. Illnesses such as peptic ulcers, migraine headaches, hypertension (or high blood pressure), bronchial asthma, colitis, and even rheumatoid arthritis have all been diagnosed in the main to be psychosomatic, that is, having their roots in the emotions rather than in physical disorders.

A gynecologist friend of mine once said that in his opinion 70 to 80 percent of the female problems that cause a woman to seek medical help from physicians are psychosomatic in origin, and that almost all of those problems had the emotion of anger strongly associated with them. In this dysfunctional way of handling anger the patient has learned to repress his or her anger only to have it show up later in the form of physical illness.

When it comes to mishandling anger, we Christians are past masters at handling it through psychosomatic illness. I would predict, although there's no way it can be proven, that of all of the dysfunctional ways of handling anger, the most sincere and committed Christians use this method. Why? Because of all the methods, it is the least obvious. It is the most unconsciously subtle. We don't have permission to be angry or to express our anger outwardly, but we do have permission to go to bed with a migraine headache, to pop pills because of high blood pressure, or to sit on the toilet for hours because of colitis. Of all of the strategies, psychosomatic illness is the most subtle but it makes the least sense when viewed practically.

Passive–Aggressive Behavior

The last strategy for mishandling anger that I'd like to mention is what psychologists have labeled "passive–aggressive" behavior. The passive–aggressive person never gets angry, he only gets even. The key is in understanding the label. First of all, the anger is dealt with passively rather than actively. For example, if he gets angry with you, you know it but you can't really pin him with it. He can always weasel out. The only way you know he's angry is that he gets you later in a back door kind of way. In its simplest form it sometimes comes across as criticism. The husband who is refused sex by his wife the night before handles it passively aggressively when he comes home the next day and complains loudly that he's "sick and tired of hamburger every night." He didn't get angry the night before, he just gets even.

In another form it comes across as habitual lateness or tardiness. The wife who has the responsibility of getting both herself and the children ready for church on Sunday morning while her husband impatiently waits, reading the paper, handles her anger passively aggressively when she finds herself carefully and slowly putting on her makeup while her husband and the children sit in the car with engine running and horn blasting. She doesn't get angry, she just gets even. It is the employee who deliberately slows his production to get back at a supervisor who has criticized his work. The forms vary but the net result is always the same. They don't get angry, they just get even.

The treatment of patients who are passive–aggressive is genuinely discouraging, and living with them is a thousand times more painful. They'll typically agree with everything you say. On the surface they couldn't appear to be more cooperative. But when they leave the office, at the unconscious level they set out to defeat you. They just never get around to changing. They make promise after promise to their aggrieved spouse but they never get around to doing anything about it. They don't get angry; they just never keep their promises. The spouse is often caught in a terrible bind. Make demands and they'll agree on the surface while at the same time beneath the surface they'll work to defeat those same demands. Don't make demands and they'll just stay the same, more passive than ever. When you're married to a passive–aggressive person it seems you never win. You continually feel defeated but you can't really figure out how. Of all the dysfunctional mishandlings of anger, the passive–aggressive personality is the most difficult to treat using traditional therapy. Those whom I have seen change, and there have been a few, did so because of the clear and direct intervention of the Holy Spirit. With God all things are possible. A step in the right direction for the person who is passive–aggressive is to admit to himself or herself that he is mishandling his anger, and to begin working on more constructive ways of dealing with his emotion.

Most of us at one time or another in our lives have probably used all of these ways of mishandling anger. The typical response of some of us, having had them catalogued, is to become discouraged, feeling that to change would be impossible. I only mention this because many of us seem to look for ways, albeit unconsciously, to downgrade ourselves. We are quick to see the "beam" in our eye before we see the "mote" elsewhere. We reverse the scriptural teaching. To react that way would be exactly the opposite of what I would hope. I have included this catalogue only to give each of us a means for looking at ourselves objectively. Only when we begin to see ourselves accurately will we be able to do anything about the way or ways we mishandle anger. It's the "truth" that will set us free, no matter how much it hurts. We must not be afraid of the truth.

Managing Our Anger

Having inventoried our behaviorial responses to anger, what remains is to establish a scriptural pattern for managing the emotion. If God is truly the architect of the human spirit, he certainly knows how we function and, because he is a God of grace, he would not leave us without directions for handling our emotions. Although the Bible is not an exhaustive book of instructions on mental health, I believe there are principles in its pages that will help lead us to a more positive personal psychology, a practical, constructive way of dealing with ourselves, especially our emotions.

As I stated earlier in this chapter, the first step in the establishment of a positive strategy for managing our anger is to recognize the legitimate, God-given character of the emotion. Anger is as valid as is joy, or hope, or any of the other emotions we are able to experience as human beings. What makes anger ungodly is our failure to control it or its abuse. Anger is probably the easiest of our emotions to abuse. More so than any other, it can wreak havoc upon the recipients. That it is so easily abused only magnifies the need for establishing a positive means for controlling it. Why do I say that anger is, or can be, a positive God-given emotion? The evidence for my statement is in the Scripture itself, and in the very nature and character of God himself.

In the first place the Scripture records the fact that men of God throughout the ages have evidenced the emotion of anger. Moses, David, Nehemiah, the prophets, all experienced anger. The Old Testament is full of illustrations of men who experienced this emotion, as is the New Testament. However, it is not the human illustrations that should guide and determine our thinking. Where we must look ultimately is to the Lord Jesus himself. How did Jesus handle this emotion? In particular, two passages of Scripture stand out. The first is in Mark's Gospel.

> Again he entered the synagogue, and a man was there who had a withered hand. And they watched him, to see whether he would heal him on the sabbath, so that they might accuse him. And he said to the man who had the withered hand, "Come here." And he said to them, "Is it lawful on the sabbath to do good or to do harm, to save life or to kill?" But they were silent. And he looked around at them with anger, grieved at their hardness of heart, and said to the man, "Stretch out your hand." He stretched it out, and his hand was restored (Mark 3:1–5 RSV).

Jesus, when confronted with the unbelief of the Pharisees, "looked around at them *with anger*, grieved at their hardness of heart." Jesus got angry. There's no avoiding it. There are purists, however, who would try to redefine his emotion and make it "righteous indignation." My response to them is that they are explaining away the clear meaning of Scripture and making it obscure. The word used by Mark in this passage is the Greek word *orge*, a word used to describe the strongest of all passions.* I'm convinced that the same physiological processes that course through your body when you get angry were coursing through Jesus' body as he faced the Pharisees. To deny that he got angry is to play word games and to force Jesus to the less than fully human. What makes him believable is that he was tested in all points as we are, "yet without sin" (Heb. 4:15). He could feel what he felt, and he could react the way in which he reacted "yet without sin." The critical issue for you and for me, therefore, is not the presence of the emotion of anger but how can we, like Jesus, deal with that emotion "without sin"?

Jesus and Anger

The second passage of Scripture that would seem to me to be of relevance in any discussion of the legitimacy of anger is found in John's Gospel:

> The Passover of the Jews was at hand, and Jesus went up to Jerusalem. In the temple he found those who were selling oxen and sheep and pigeons, and the money–changers at their business. And making a whip of cords, he drove them all, with the sheep and oxen, out of the temple; and he poured out the coins of the money–changers and overturned their tables. And he told them who sold the pigeons, "Take these things away; you shall not make my Father's house a house of trade. His disciples remembered that it was written, "Zeal for thy house will consume me" (John 2:13–17 RSV).

---

*W. E. Wine, *Expository Dictionary of New Testament Words*, Vol. I, pp. 55–56, has an excellent discussion of the meaning of the word and its use in the New Testament.

This passage is the clearest example of Jesus' experience of anger. It records that he cleansed the Temple because of the abuses that had come to characterize Pharisaical worship. The essential issue for our discussion has to do with his state of mind when he took his scourge of cords and drove the violators out. Whatever he felt, it was an emotion that consumed him in the sense it commanded his physical presence at the time (the meaning of the word "zeal" in verse 17). Any fair evaluation would have to admit that Jesus was angry and that his emotion caused him to react strongly. John's description is of a totally involved, impassioned person, a man who experienced his emotions, "yet without sin."

Not only did this emotion called anger characterize Jesus at times, it also characterizes the very nature of God the Father in this present age. He is angry with the Jews nationally (Rom. 9:22; 1 Thess. 2:16). He is angry with those who disobey the Lord Jesus (John 3:36). And as the Judge of this present world he is angry, in the here and now with those who live according to the error of this world rather than the truth of his kingdom (Rom. 1:18, 3:5, 12:19, Eph. 5:6).

Whatever this emotion called anger is, it must be valid and legitimate. For it to be less so invalidates the nature and character of the Lord Jesus and God the Father, himself.

Processing Our Anger

This brings me to the third dimension for establishing a biblical strategy for managing our anger, a constructive methodology for processing the emotion. I'd like to suggest that such a methodology should include three principles or "rules of thumb" when it comes to working through our feelings. These three principles, I believe, can be inferred from Paul's letter to the Ephesians:

> Therefore, putting away falsehood, let every one speak the truth with his neighbor, for we are members one of another. Be angry but do not sin; do not let the sun go down on your anger (Eph. 4:25, 26 RSV).

The first rule of thumb I would suggest is that the emotion of *anger should be handled assertively and not aggressively*. Handling my anger assertively involves speaking the "truth" (v. 25). It involves taking the responsibility for my own feelings rather than making others responsible for them. I can tell I'm being assertive when I am using "I" statements rather than "you" statements. Unfortunately we have been taught that the use of the pronoun "I" automatically infers selfishness. Sometimes it is exactly the opposite. The use of the pronoun "you" can be the most selfish mode of communication that I can use. Suppose for example I am angry with my wife. I can accuse her by saying "You don't really care for me. All you're really concerned about is yourself." At my house, that kind of accusation either from me or from Lucy would bring about a quick denial and probably would lead to defensiveness. Why defensiveness? Because the "you statements" are really forms of aggressive behavior and people get defensive when they're attacked.

On the other hand, if I am angry, I can say, "I'm

feeling neglected and left out." The difference in tone to the two statements is the difference between "I" statements and "You" statements. Too often we wad our words up like clubs and hit each other over the head with them only to wonder later why things got so badly out of hand. That's why "you" can be so brutal. "Truth" involves my talking about only that which I know to be so. When it comes to anger I probably only really "know" about how "*I feel*" and not about "*what you are.*" Paul says that I am to tell you the truth, that is, I am to assert myself rather than to act aggressively toward you.

The second rule of thumb is that I am to handle my anger daily and not store it up for more than twenty–four hours. The Scripture is obvious at this point. "Do not let the sun go down on your anger" (Eph. 4:26). It's interesting that Paul uses a strengthened form of the Greek word for anger in the second half of the verse. In so doing he probably is drawing attention not only to the anger itself but also to the provocation of that anger. In other words, he is saying that we are to process both the emotion and the causes for that emotion *every day*.

I have already suggested that at least three ways of mishandling anger involve repressing the emotion under the guise of dealing with it later, if at all. Depression, psychosomatic illness, and passive–aggressive behavior are all clear–cut ways of putting off handling anger. The wisdom of God is that the emotion is to be handled in the "here and now" rather than putting it off.

A number of times I have suggested to my patients that they need to learn how to argue and that there needs to be a different pattern of conflict in their relationship. Usually they look at me as if I had lost my mind. The whole pattern of their relationship is usually characterized by hostility, bitterness, or isolation and withdrawal. However, I'm not suggesting that they make things worse. Quite the opposite. It's a fact that many of us store up our angers for days, weeks, months, and years at a time. When we finally process the emotion because it can be denied no longer, it comes rushing forth in giant torrents, sweeping everything and everybody before its path with little or no regard for the consequences. It is also a fact borne out in relationship after relationship that when we handle our angers daily, they won't build up inside us and the conflict levels in our relationships will diminish rather than increase. We are to grow to a point where we try to keep current in the processing of our emotions. We are to be moving to a place where we can trust each other not to be carrying excess emotional baggage from the past. What a free feeling it is to know that when the sun comes up it truly is a new day.

The third rule of thumb I would suggest is, in my opinion, the most important. Anger is not only to be handled assertively and daily; *it is to be handled deliberately and not impulsively.* For the longest time I couldn't for the life of me figure out how Jesus processed his anger any differently than I process mine until I came to see that his anger was expressed only after a long and patient ordeal. He had been systematically rejected and subjected to ridicule by the Pharisees from the time he began his public ministry. His offer to be their King had been legitimate. He had gone out of his way to be sure that they had every opportunity to accept his offer of the kingdom, but their rejection was definite and total. They wanted nothing to do with him. Only after constant provocation did his anger show. He had "counted ten" many times over.

Jay Kesler, President of Youth for Christ International, refers to this process as a "response interval." It means that whenever I become aware of the emotion of anger I am to automatically put my response mechanism in neutral until I have had an opportunity to think it through. Will my response make sense in light of the offense? Nehemiah mirrored just such a response interval in the Old Testament when he said, "I was very angry when I heard their cry and these words. *Then I consulted with myself,* and I rebuked the nobles . . ." (Neh. 5:6,7). Much of our anger becomes destructive when we impulsively blast off and "let it all hang out." That's one of the problems of both stamp–saving and scapegoating. Whoever gets caught in the middle of the explosion catches the brunt of our wrath. The object is to learn to think it through and be "slow to anger" (James 1:19).

Having said all this, I realize that many of us could read it and go on living and reacting as we always have in the past. We still will not have been able to think through "why" we get angry. Why is it that we feel rejected? Why do we get so defensive? We need something more in order to really get at the core of our emotion, to get at the "why?" Something to do during the "response interval."

A—H—E—N

Contemporary psychology has suggested a process that I have found to be of help to me personally as well as to my patients. For the sake of my own understanding I have renamed some of the process. The process is called A—H—E—N. The four letters stand for Anger, Hurt, Expectation, and Need. They represent a process by which you can reason your way back through your anger to its roots.

The process assumes that *behind every anger is hurt*. Have you ever had someone say to you, "I'm not angry. I'm just hurt"? They're probably right. They just haven't let the emotional process go far or long enough. If you'll remember the passage where Jesus was said to look at the Pharisees with anger, you'll remember that the verse also said that he was *"grieved at their hardness of heart"* (Mark 3:5). He was hurt. And so it is with our anger most of the time. The reason we are upset is that somehow we are personally affected to the point where our physical body reacts in such a way as to protect itself from being hurt.

But what's behind the hurt? Usually it's some *expectation* I have that has not been met, and behind that expectation is a *need* that I either consciously or unconsciously have. The expectation in the case of Jesus was his hope that they would respond to his offer of the kingdom. In his case, the need is more difficult to determine. Perhaps it had to do with his awareness of what was expected of him. We do know that he was disappointed over Israel's rejection of his offer of the kingdom. The disappointment was real as evidenced by the grief he demonstrated when he wept over Jerusalem (Luke 13:34 ff.). We also know that he took his responsibilities seriously and that he, being human, would have felt their rejection and only he would have comprehended its full weight. Whatever the reason, there were needs that underpinned his expectations.

In the case of Jesus, his needs are difficult to identify. But, when I get angry, the needs are not so hard to pin down. The process of A—H—E—N has been useful to me on several occasions. For example, for the life of me I couldn't figure out why I would get so angry with my wife whenever she was more than a few minutes late coming home. It didn't make sense until I was able to reason on my way back through the process and get to my basic needs.

If Lucy would be no more than twenty to thirty minutes late, I would begin a very gruesome ritual in my mind. First of all, I would picture her in an accident wrapped around some telephone pole or I would imagine her car in a terrible wreck on the freeway. The next step in my mind would be the police at the door and then the hospital, and so on. By the time she actually pulled in the driveway, absolutely unaware of my panic and oblivious of my fantasies, I would burst out the front door and confront her with, "Where have you been? I have been worried sick. Why didn't you call?" (Note that in three sentences I have two "you" statements.) Quite legitimately, she would get defensive and off we'd go on one of our patented quarrels.

Finally I decided to take my own advice and figure out what was going on. I would be hurt that she wouldn't call even though we'd never agreed that she should. Still, I had the expectation that she should be more sensitive and conscientious and protect me from such hurt. Not until I was able to get behind the expectation to my need was I able to understand my anger. In my lifetime several very close loved ones have died unexpectedly. When I was a child, my father died. When I was a teen–ager, my cousin and my grandfather died without warning. As an adult, I heard the news of my own child's death from my wife over the telephone. Psychologically I carry a dread inside that whoever I really love will be taken from me quite suddenly. It was this need that Lucy was bumping into. Only when I was able to tell her about it was she able to understand and make adjustments. Now she calls if she's to be more than a half–hour late and the quarrels are gone. We were able to work it through. Now I don't have to be angry anymore.

So it is with anger. It's there. It's real and it's valid. Only when we accept it and do something with it are we able to get rid of it. My concern for the Christian community is that we have learned to deal with the emotion altogether too destructively. And in the destructiveness of the process we are bound by our emotions rather than free. My prayer for all of us is that we learn to be "free to be angry," and then we shall be on the way to being "free indeed."

5

Free to Be Responsible for Yourself

Free to Be Responsible for Yourself

Anxiety. The dictionary defines the word as the "state of being uneasy, apprehensive, or worried about what may happen; misgiving." To the student who is writing a term paper in his beginning psychology class, this definition may be sufficient. But to the one who is anxious, it is not. To the person who is suffering through an anxiety attack, it is like walking through the valley of the shadow of death. Everything in him cries out that words like "uneasy," "apprehensive," or "worry" are poor substitutes for the pain of reality.

Several people who have described themselves to me as being "anxious" have said that their pain, the emotional pain attached to this malady, is worse than any physical pain they have ever suffered. I have had patients tell me they would willingly trade their anxiety state and the life style that goes with it for any number of terrible physical ailments. Often the pain that comes from within seems far worse than they can bear, and what's more when they're in the midst of it they're certain it will never end.

111

Anxiety and the Christian

I have also noticed that anxiety and the pain that goes with it is especially tormenting to Christians. Please take careful note of exactly what I'm saying. I'm *not* saying that Christians are especially tormented by anxiety. I am saying that Christians, when they find themselves in an anxiety state, find that state to be unusually burdensome. Why would this be so? My observation is that Christians too often back themselves into a corner through the misapplication of some very popular verses found in Scripture, especially in the apostle Paul's letter to the Philippians, chapter 4, verses 6 and 7: "Have no anxiety about anything, but in everything by prayer and supplication with thanksgiving let your requests be made known to God. And the peace of God, which passes all understanding, will keep your hearts and your minds in Christ Jesus" (RSV). Practically speaking, what was Paul teaching his readers?

Many interpret the verse in a way that is close to condemnation. When they find themselves reacting anxiously to their world, they judge and berate themselves. The verses are taken to mean, "Don't you ever, ever let yourselves be anxious." I don't think that's what Paul meant at all. I think he meant to be comforting and supportive of those who find themselves being overcome by the misgivings of life. Paul's intent was not to condemn but to comfort and to instruct. Quoting the verse and telling myself or others that we "shouldn't be anxious" rarely helps. In fact, my experience is the exact opposite. Judgment and condemnation simply add to, rather than detract from, anxiety.

But just exactly what is anxiety and how do you cope with it when you need to? To understand this state of mind an illustration will be helpful. On a Friday afternoon I was in my office having finished a busy week. It had been a good week and I was finishing it off bone tired. I had one more patient and my week was over. The patient was a young man with whom I had worked for several weeks. His emotional state had been deterioriating rapidly to the point where he was barely able to function. Earlier in the afternoon his wife had called with an emergency message. Her husband was stranded in the parking lot where he worked and he, because of anxiety, was unable to start the car let alone drive home. For all intents and purposes he had ceased functioning. She was on her way to get him and would I please try to work him into my schedule before I left for home? I had a cancellation and she desperately grasped the open appointment. She would not be alone and she would not be forced to carry the burden by herself.

When her husband walked into my office his face was flushed, his breathing came in short gasps as he physically collapsed into the chair. I waited without saying a word. At first his response was to glare at me accusingly. Finally he burst out at me, "What's going to happen to me? Am I going crazy? When are you going to make this stop? I can't stand it anymore. I'd rather be dead than to live this way. Can't you do something?"

Listening to his plea for help brought a response in me that I have learned to monitor. Everything inside me wanted to relieve him of his pain. He obviously wasn't kidding and his pain was real. Was I or was I not a "healer"? Was I or was I not a competent therapist? The tendency for those of us who are in the helping professions is to let ourselves become caught in the trap where the responsibility for healing becomes ours rather than the patient's. It's easy for a therapist, a counselor, or anyone else offering help to play god in a person's life and to become the all–knowing, all–powerful source of wisdom, dispensing the elixir of truth to those who anxiously drink it.

This time, however, I avoided my typical error. I purposely left the responsibility where it belonged, on his shoulders. There was little I could do beyond offering support and seeing to it that medication from his family physician was being used properly.

"I can't make you well," I answered. "That's not my job."

A look of panic and disbelief swept over his face.

"Well, for God's sake, if you won't then what am I going to do? What have I been paying you all this money for?" His voice shuddered and he buried his face in his hands. He was like a small child who brings his badly skinned knee to his parent with the full expectation that the parent will respond and patch him up. He is accustomed to having others become responsible for him rather than being responsible for himself. That's exactly where the problem lay with my patient. He was reacting to his world like a small child and he was habitually in search of a parent to take care of him. His anxiety was the result of the helpless, hopeless, dependent child inside, crying out for someone to take care of him.

I find this pattern to be customarily present in those who are suffering from severe anxiety. Oftentimes the anxiety–ridden are like small, lost children desperately wishing for someone to come along and rescue them from their plight, only to find that they are soon lost again in another place and at another time. When I confront someone who is suffering from anxiety with this tendency, their typical reaction is one of anger. Later they usually admit that it is true.

My next response to the young man in my office may seem brutal on the surface, but it was chosen according to a deliberate plan. In my very best clinical voice I said, "All right. Why don't you have one?"

"Have what?" he replied.

"Go ahead and have a nervous breakdown."

"Do what?" he screamed.

"Go ahead and have a nervous breakdown. But let's get it over with before five o'clock. If you take any longer I'll be late for dinner. And, if you wait longer than that you'll probably ruin my weekend."

He couldn't believe his ears.

"You can't mean that. You can't just tell me to fall apart on command. You make it sound like that's what I want."

"Well, I don't know who's going to keep you from it if you're not. I certainly can't. I've already told you. That's not my job."

The rage shuddered in his voice.

"You, you, you can't treat me that way."

I said, "Well, look. If you've decided in your head to have a nervous breakdown, and you're through struggling against it, and you're ready to give in, there's really nothing I can do. You've made up your mind, so let's get it over with."

He roared to his feet and stormed around the room. His only hope of "parental" care and comfort was deserting him and he was completely alone. Until that time he had planned on me being his emotional back-up. If he couldn't cope with life then I would cope for him. He had come to the end of his rope.

I then began a careful program of confrontation and instruction.

"I want you to know that I care about you and I'm sorry that you're hurting. But I also know that you've been trying, and succeeding, for weeks to put the responsibility for your getting well on my shoulders. As long as you're trying to throw off the responsibility for yourself onto somebody else, you're just never going to get well. In fact, the worst thing I could do right now is to take the responsibility for your emotional health."

At that moment he came to a decision point where he had to make a choice. Was he or was he not going to try to break a lifelong habit of making others responsible for him? He was a long term "emotional leaner" who had never faced the fact that inside he was a dependent child and that his dependency was robbing him of his ability to function, the ability to enjoy life as a grown man, an adult.

Let me digress for a brief moment to discuss what I think is a related misapplication of Scripture, one that contributes dramatically to the whole problem of anxiety, worry, and so on. This was directly relevant to the young man in my office.

It is a fact that Jesus said ". . . unless you turn and become like children, you will never enter the kingdom of God" (Matt. 18.3 RSV). These are qualities that seem to encourage a kind of dependency. It is also a fact that the Apostle Paul exhorted the Christian to exhibit qualities such as endurance, hardness, and self-discipline, qualities hardly present in "dependent" children. On the surface these teachings would seem to contradict each other. In the arena of life the sincere Christian finds himself in the bind of trying to fulfill two seemingly opposite instructions. The problem is further complicated by those who are emotional leaners. On the one hand they take the words of Jesus to justify their dependency and on the other they struggle with, or conveniently ignore, the teachings that exhort them to maturity and adulthood.

Trust and Dependency

An answer to the dilemma lies in the recognition of the difference between two words, trust and dependency. Trust is the ability to abandon oneself freely into the custody of another. Dependency is the clinging quality of relying on another for existence. The critical distinction as far as I'm concerned is in the word "clinging." It is possible to trust another without clinging to him. In fact, the act of clinging, in my opinion, indicates the absence of trust.

Jesus encouraged his followers to evidence a quality of trust, that is, an abandonment of their person to him as Lord. He did not encourage a state of dependency in which he became responsible for their existence. They still had to work, to be responsible for their food and shelter. The balance between the two is the key. It is possible to trust without becoming a dependent person.

There is a second important issue to be discussed in this distinction between trust and dependency. It has to do with the issue of control or power. Dependency appears on the surface to be an act of yielding to another but in reality it is usually an attempt to gain control over the person. The anxious, dependent person who is in the habit of making others responsible for him is often engaged in a power play. If I can make you responsible for me, responsible for keeping me alive, I have control of you. Let me illustrate.

The most powerful person in the world is the newborn infant. He can dominate his mother as no one else can. A helpless child who can't take care of himself dominates his mother's life. In the middle of the night if he cries long and loud enough he can usually get his mother to come and minister to his needs. Others can call in the middle of the night, they can cajole and plead yet the same mother will exercise restraint and judgment and come only if she thinks she's really needed. The infant derives his power over his mother from his dependency upon her, from her absolute responsibility for him.

So it is with the emotional leaner, the anxious, dependent person. In successfully foisting off responsibility for himself onto others he succeeds in gaining control over the one who either knowingly or unknowingly has taken that responsibility.

It's appropriate for an infant to be dependent and helpless. But in the normal course of growing up we are supposed to assume more and more responsibility for ourselves. By the time we are adults it's appropriate that we function autonomously and independently of others, not relying upon them for the maintenance of life.

Here is where the tension lies for the Christian: having the freedom to be independent and autonomous while at the same time being free enough to trust and abandon ourselves to Christ. My observation is that the worried, anxious, fretful individual is not really able to do either and often feels frustrated as a result. The question is whether or not a way through the problem of anxiety exists. I think there is. It lies in the freedom Christ provides when he sets us free.

The principles found in a single verse of Scripture are preeminently useful in the treatment of anxiety and worry. These principles have been used by God to set people free, free from the chains of anxiety. The verse is found in the apostle Paul's second letter to young Timothy, chapter 1, verse 7: ". . . for God did not give us the spirit of timidity but a spirit of power, and love and self-control" (RSV).

The word used by Paul that is translated "timidity" is a word whose meaning in the original Greek is cowardice. It has to do with the feeling of helplessness and hopelessness that ends in timidity. The word connotes a "cowering in the corner" kind of attitude toward life. It is the spectacle of a young man stranded in a parking lot unable to drive home and dependent upon his wife to come and take care of him. It's the way many of us have felt at one time or another in our lives.

According to the apostle Paul, God's prescription for worry and anxiety is threefold. It involves "power," "love," and "self–control."

The "Power" Approach

The first ingredient I have found useful in combating anxiety has to do with "power" or what I have come to refer to as *an assertive rather than a passive approach toward life*. Paul is obviously not referring to muscle power or even intellectual power. Paul was referring to the capacity to stand up, turn around, and push against one's environment. The power not to be swept away helplessly by the forces of life. It is the determination to say, "I will not give in." It involves at times the digging in of our heels, a resistance to compromise, either with ourselves or with others.

"Power" is what Martin Luther demonstrated when he singlehandedly launched the Reformation. Whether you are Catholic or Protestant you have to admire the pluckish tenacity of a man who would stand against his entire environment and social system. That's "power." Had it been left to many of us we would have never done what Luther did, not because we don't agree with the issues, but because we would be unwilling to stand alone against the tide, a willingness to take the heat.

While Luther is a dramatic example, there are others closer to home who come to mind. For example, God used this willingness to be assertive rather than passive toward life at one time to turn my life around and to launch me in a new direction.

The occasion was the arrival of my wife and me at seminary. Like many young student couples, our plans were for me to go to school and study full time and for my wife to work and put me through school. The four seminary years were neatly planned and laid out before us. But since the "best laid plans of mice and men go oft astray" it didn't work that way. Immediately into our first semester my wife became pregnant with our first child and the pregnancy forced a reappraisal of our plans. My first instincts were to "trust the Lord" for our future. He would provide. "Trusting the Lord" involved my settling back waiting for a check in the mail that would cover the expenses of the semester. Nothing happened. Weeks went by with no money. Where was God? I comforted myself that he was obviously waiting so as to test our faith.

As my wife increased with child so did my anxiety. As my anxiety increased so did the pressure. Finally, after months of waiting around I got the picture. If I was going to be able to stay in school and still provide for my family I was going to have to find a job. Like most people I dreaded the process of job hunting. I had no choice, so I hit the pavement. Again weeks went by with no success. Now anxiety turned to desperation tinged with resentment. God was letting me down. I secretly laid plans to drop out of school and forget my plans for vocational Christian service. It was at this point that the situation changed dramatically. It didn't involve my going to the mailbox and miraculously finding a check from some unknown source, the miracle I had prayed for. What it did involve was the provision of a job, a job working in a juvenile detention home, a job that opened a whole new field of ministry up to me, the field of psychology and family education. I held that job through our entire seminary career. Our needs were met and the added benefit of a new direction to our lives was added.

I have since had occasion to reflect upon that time in our lives and have come to realize that much of my problem stemmed from my belief that the exercise of faith is equivalent to passivity, that is, trusting in God involves doing nothing. If you do something it can't be faith. I don't believe that now, nor do I live my life that way. Neither do I encourage others to live their lives that way. God most often directs us when we are moving and active, when we have taken the initiative. It is the assertion of oneself into the mainstream of life that provides alternatives, when doors are opened and closed. I think this is what Paul means when he says that God has given us "power."

If you find yourself at a place in your life marked by anxiety, worry, or indecision, assert yourself! Do something! Stand up and move out! The gnawing apprehension that saps us of hope is handled only through the assertive making of decisions and the action that naturally follows.

In summary, those who are plagued with worry and anxiety are faced with a decision: to develop an assertive rather than a passive attitude toward their lives and to accept the responsibility for themselves that naturally flows from that decision.

The "Love" Approach

The second ingredient I have found to be useful in combating anxiety is what I like to think of as a *"giving to others" approach to life.*

There are four words used in the ancient Greek that are translated into the English word love, two of which are used in the New Testament. The two used in the New Testament are *philia*, friendship love, and *agape*, self–sacrificing love. It is this latter kind of love that Paul uses in his letter to Timothy. Evidently, there is a relationship between overcoming timidity (anxiety), and sacrificial love for others (agape).

Think of it this way. An infant helplessly lying in his crib is supremely conscious of his needs and is completely oblivious to the needs of others. When he cries he's usually saying "I'm hungry," or "change my diapers." "I don't care what time of night it is or whether or not you're tired. I've got a rash and I hurt." He is preeminently occupied with his own pain and discomfort.

That's the way it is sometimes with those who are struggling with anxiety and worry. They easily become entangled in their own pain and discomfort to the point of becoming oblivious to others. They are overwhelmed with their own "rash."

It was so with the young man in my office. While he was struggling with his anxiety, his own family was falling apart. His wife had reached the end of her rope and was near the point of physical exhaustion. She was completely responsible for the maintenance of the family, both emotionally and physically. The children were misbehaving in school, wetting the bed at home, and in general, falling apart. The young man was out of touch with the torment around him. He was completely focused on himself.

Remaining faithful to my treatment plan I asked him, "What about the other people in your life? What about their pain? I know you're hurting but maybe they are, too."

His first instinct was to brush my inquiry aside as irrelevant. "Well, they've got their problems, but that will all clear up once we've solved what's wrong with me." His answer was predictable. He gave the appearance of caring but in reality he was only concerned about himself.

I wasn't about to let him off the hook.

"Can you function and give to your family in the midst of your pain? Can you reach out and love somebody even when you're hurting?"

The look on his face went blank. I was asking him to do something he had not even thought of, let alone considered as possible. He had so long focused upon himself that he had lost the ability to see the needs of others.

If he could focus upon someone else, even for a moment, he would, of necessity be forced not to focus upon himself.

To love in the "agape" sense of the word, a self-sacrificing kind of love, sometimes involves throwing yourself into the breach of life and doing what someone else needs when everything in you is demanding the exact opposite. It involves screening out the noise of your own pain while at the same time tuning in to the soft, muffled cries of others. Somehow, in the process of refocusing the attention from yourself to others, a change takes place. The pain is not as demanding and the needs of others become clearer.

I asked again, "Is there anyone whom you think is asking for your love?" The question forced him to take inventory. "Is there somebody you can reach out to?"

His response was immediate. His eyes clouded with tears and his choked response came back, "My son."

"What does he need from you that he's not getting?" I asked.

"I guess he just needs me to spend time with him."

He was beginning to refocus.

"He keeps bugging me to play ball with him like I used to, but I've just not been able to because of the anxiety."

"Even though you're hurting, wouldn't that be a practical way of showing your love for him?" I pushed for a decision. "Will you commit yourself to go home and play ball with him, just like he's asking?"

His response was barely audible. "I'll try."

He left my office unsure and unsteady.

He returned the next week eager to let me know how his commitment had worked out.

"You know, it was really something. I was throwing the ball back and forth with my son, even though I was screaming inside, and I looked over and I saw my boy. He was playing catch with his dad. Something we hadn't done for months. My son was feeling good about me and I was doing for him just like you suggested. And then I realized, my pain didn't hurt as much."

The young man, husband and father, was on his way back. He was regaining the ability to see the needs of others. Love, a giving of yourself for others, was making a difference.

Self–Control and Self–Discipline

Even though assertiveness and love are important, these qualities, in and of themselves, are not enough. There is a necessary third ingredient, self–control or self–discipline, *an attitude of saying "no" to yourself and a willingness to live with the discomfort of your decision.*

Returning to the analogy of the dependent child fussing in his crib, we expect him to be ill–disciplined. It's entirely normal for him to be in diapers, completely lacking the ability to control his urination or bowels. There comes a time, however, when it is appropriate for a child to have matured to the point where he is able to control his own toilet habits. Anything less is inappropriate. Self–discipline in this area of life is socially expected.

126

It's of interest to me that the apostle Paul encouraged Timothy to cope with his timidity or anxiety by reminding him that he had been blessed with self-control or self-discipline. What this means to me in a very practical sense is that I can't expect God to control something in my own life that he has already given me the capacity to control for myself. That's just another way of saying he expects me to be responsible for myself. I can't lay it off on him. The relationship between self-discipline and anxiety is as follows. I have suggested that anxiety stems in part from feelings of helplessness and hopelessness. The natural consequence of helplessness and hopelessness is to try to make someone else responsible for the maintenance of life. Self-discipline is at the other end of the continuum. Self-discipline implies a mastery of self, the dominion over your own body and person.

In contrast, those who suffer from anxiety often characterize their feelings as being "out of control." No one, least of all the person himself, is really in charge. The "out-of-controlness" dramatically adds to the helplessness.

The necessary third ingredient in the treatment of anxiety is a willingness to say "no" to yourself and to live with the discomfort that usually follows. I normally ask my patients to take responsibility for some area of their life that they feel is out of control. It may be diet, physical exercise, or anything else that they will see as symbolic in their fight against anxiety. Once they do so, and once they embark upon a program of self-discipline, dramatic improvement occurs. The improvement probably happens because in the process of saying "no" to themselves and living with the discomfort that follows they, unconsciously, begin to say "no" to the pain caused by their anxiety. The control of one area of life opens the door to control in others. The sense of mastery that begins to build inside has an erasing effect upon the feelings of helplessness. Paul's encouragement to Timothy to combat timidity with self–discipline really works.

I began this chapter with the description of a malady that is intensely painful. It is the disease of anxiety, and its lesser cousin, worry. I have also suggested that when we are loosed from our sins through faith in Jesus Christ there can be a loosening of the chains of fear and anxiety. However, freedom does not always imply ease. In this case it implies work. To be free in Christ is to be free to take responsibility for ourselves and to be free of the deadening pale of helplessness and the anxiety and worry that so often follows.

6

Free to Be Demonstrative

Free to Be Demonstrative

As is the case of most days in South Vietnam, the day was hot and sticky. I was in that country on business, sent there by World Vision International to survey the possibilities of a cooperative effort placing orphaned Vietnamese children in Christian homes in the United States. The streets of Saigon were crowded with bicycles, automobiles, and the ever–present motorcycle. The sounds of war were silent but the sights of war were everywhere. Sand–filled bunkers were at every major intersection. Armed patrols stood guard at the entrances of every major building. Convoys of military trucks blasted their air–horns while they roared through the city, the rest of the populace scrambling to get out of their way or be run over.

My agenda for the day was to go with one of the World Vision staff to visit the orphanages of Saigon. I had heard stories of the victims of the war in southeast Asia, but somehow, I had never allowed the truth of those stories to touch me personally. In fact, I wasn't affected until we visited our third orphanage.

We had driven into the distant suburbs of Saigon and had parked our car on the rutted, dusty street. The noises of the city were everywhere. Vendors were hawking their wares, half–clothed little boys were playing as if nothing in their world were wrong, and the neighborhood people stared as we walked through the gates of the orphanage, a place where Americans rarely visited.

Inside the orphanage, we were greeted by the director of the orphanage, a Vietnamese Catholic Sister who offered us tea. The social amenities were pleasant. I found the Sister to be warm, gracious, and dedicated to her task. I couldn't help but notice an aura of apology that seemed to tinge her conversation. She seemed embarrassed and at first I passed it off as typical Asian humility, or the appearance of humility. The theme of her apology was the overcrowded conditions of the orphanage and her overworked staff. We reassured her that we understood and with that reassurance she assigned us to one of the junior sisters and we began our visit. I wasn't ready for what I was to see.

Everywhere there were children, thousands of them, neat, relatively clean, and like children everywhere, laughing and playing. My heart warmed to them and they shyly responded to my attention. One little boy in particular took me by the hand and became my companion for the rest of our stay. We visited building after building beginning with the oldest children and proceeding to the youngest. My spirits were high until we came to the infants' nursery.

The place was clean by Asian standards and the small cribs were lined up side by side, row after row. The visual impact of seeing hundreds of babies all in one room, some sleeping, most crying, overwhelmed me. The smell of urine filled the room as I looked around to see who was caring for the children. The staff for that nursery consisted of just two young Vietnamese attendants who, working at a steady pace, were able to feed and change the diapers of the babies probably only twice a day. The rest of the time the babies lay there, staring at the ceiling or at the slats in their cribs. There were obviously more children than could be taken care of. Some had to suffer.

I began a slow, deliberate walk up and down each of the rows. I would stop and touch one of the babies but they wouldn't respond. It was as if I didn't exist. Crib after crib, child after child, each just lay there with no response whatsoever to my presence or my touch. Half-way down one aisle I came to the crib of an infant I saw was dying. The child's breathing was labored, his eyes were glazed, and his skin was cold to the touch. I yelled out for someone to come and do something. But the attendants just shrugged their shoulders as if to say that nothing could be done. I protested to my World Vision escort but there was nothing she could do either. Babies died in that nursery every day. As I stood there and watched the baby die, I was filled with deep frustration and helplessness. I was angry at the war, and the grim reality that very little could be done. Babies died like that every day.

Why did that child die? It wasn't disease. That child died because of neglect, a neglect it seemed no one could avoid. In the three months of that child's life he had been held less than a total of eight hours. It is normal for mothers to hold, cuddle, and caress their children. In that orphanage there were no mothers and there was no caressing, no cuddling, no touching. Children need to be held and loved. When they aren't they die. If they're infants they die literally. If they're older they die, or become diseased, psychologically.

It is impossible to overestimate the importance of being held and touched in the development of an infant. In fact, some modes of contemporary psychotherapy assert that the roots of our emotional problems lie in our being deprived in our early stages of the comforts and assurances of being held and cuddled. Part of the healing process psychologically is the institution of regular and loving tactile stimulation by a parentlike figure. The rationale behind the therapy makes sense. Unfortunately, it is easily abused when it becomes another form of kinky sex–therapy, and the public as a whole and the Christian community in particular are turned off.

After I returned from Vietnam my experience in that orphanage lingered with me for months. I watched that baby die many times over in my dreams at night. I couldn't shake the emotional impact of the experience. What it did for me, however, was to awaken within me the realization that many of my patients were struggling psychologically with the same kind of void that killed that baby. They hungered inside to be loved and affirmed, to be touched.

I also became aware that most of us probably hunger for the same kind of affirmation, the need to be touched and to be held. For example, on one occasion

I observed some worshipers as they gathered at a church where I was preaching. People who obviously loved each other, who were brothers and sisters in Christ, greeted each other as if they were distant relatives. Almost all of the greeting was verbal, except for those men who shook hands. Nods of heads, "Hello, how are you's" and "I'm fine's," filled the church foyer. It was as if we were a people without hands and arms, almost without bodies. The emotional distance between the worshipers followed them into the sanctuary. The music was good, the preaching fair, and yet it was as if I were preaching to a room of disembodied spirits. We were there as a people of God but the link between us was missing. We were in the same sanctuary but we weren't together.

Why is that so? Why have we become almost solely dependent upon verbal communication in our churches? Why is it that if someone is physically demonstrative others react suspiciously? Is it the strictures of our traditions that bind us or the strictures of the Word of God?

In answer to that question, I have come to several conclusions. In the first place, I think we are bound because we have been taught that all behavior is sexual in origin. That is to say, the sexual drive underlies all that we do. If this is so, we need to suspect or be careful of any physical show of affection. Is that position biblical? Most certainly not. It is the rawest expression of Freudian psychology. According to Freud, the sexual drive, or libido, forms the most primitive and basic force in our relationships. It is the libido that struggles to be free and sets off the conflict between the id, or seat of the libido, and the super–ego, that part of the personality whose job it is to keep the id under control.

The Freudian Fraud

While I appreciate Freud and his contribution to psychology I don't agree with him that all behavior is basically sexual and I certainly don't think the body of Christ is to govern its behavior based upon anyone's psychology, let alone Sigmund Freud. We are sexual beings, but that's not all we are. When we are in Christ, the whole of our personalities can be expressed. God made us as thinking, feeling, experiential beings, all of which can be integrated into the freedom of the Christian life. To be perpetually suspect of any part is to deny that God's power can redeem and make all things new in Christ.

The second conclusion follows closely upon the first. It is that we are basically afraid of our sexuality. Either through ignorance or fear we come to think of our sexuality as some big, bad "boogy-man" lurking inside ready to roar out of our inward parts and embarrass us in front of everyone. We become afraid that if we are touched by someone or if we touch someone, we will automatically become sexually aroused and will tumble off to bed in some sort of Greek or Roman orgy. The answer to the dilemma is to accept our sexuality as being God–given and to put it in its proper place in our lives. To think of it as evil lurking in the foggy mists of our souls is to let that fear come to control us like a child's fear of ghosts keeps him awake at night.

I became aware of my own fear of my sexuality early in my career as a therapist. I had bought, hook, line and sinker, the Freudian presupposition that the therapist is never to touch his patient lest some incestuous theme be acted out and the relationship contaminated. Still I couldn't get over the fact that there were times when my patients, both men and women, need the comfort of a caring, concerned human being. I remember broaching the subject with my clinical supervisor.

"Is it ever appropriate for the therapist to touch his patient? What I mean is, will I foul things up?"

His answer hangs in my mind even today.

"My God, yes, you can touch them. You're a human being, aren't you? Are you afraid of being human?"

At the time I hadn't thought of it in terms of "being human." I was only thinking in terms of doing what was right. Since that time I have come to see touching and holding as being the normal expression of caring and concern. It is true that it can become the preamble to sexual activity but it doesn't necessarily have to be so. It's possible for it to be a part of the process of human communication, as a part of healing.

Let me give you an example. On a few occasions I have been hospitalized for minor medical reasons. The first time I was hospitalized, the hospital chaplain came by my room and greeted me. We talked for a brief time and he asked if he could pray with me. I said that he could and he stood at the foot of my bed and prayed. When he finished, I was appreciative as he said good–by and left. The next day, one of the pastors from my home church visited me. As in the case of the night before, when it came time for him to leave he asked if he could pray with me. This time, however, was different. He walked to the side of my bed, grasped my hand, and prayed. I was afraid and in need, and his touch meant as much to me as his word. The contrast between the two was dramatic and the impact of their ministry equally so.

Jesus Dared to Touch

In connection with this thought, I'm impressed with the number of times Jesus reached out and "touched" those who were in need. He touched the leper (Matt. 8:3), he touched the blind (Matt. 9:29), and he touched his disciples when they were afraid (Matt. 17:7). There was something special about his touch, and when we reach out to others there is something special about our touch as well.

The crux of what I'm trying to say is that we have been created by God as physical, tactical beings, capable of experiencing warmth and closeness through the sensation of physical touch. It is a fact that when new–born infants are deprived of being held and caressed they die or at the least are intellectually and emotionally retarded. It is my belief that we as adult human beings still need to be touched. There is a form of communication that makes sense only in the context of physical touching and affirmation. It is also a fact that Jesus made it a consistent habit to touch those who were closest to him and those to whom he ministered. And, even more personal than that, each of us can recount times when someone has reached out and touched us at a time when we were hurting. Somehow, the physical expression of their care made a difference. Something very basic in us was touched by their touching.

What I am suggesting is that when you are free in Christ, you can lay aside the fears of lurking promiscuity and latent homosexuality and respond to others as Christ would respond if he were here. I believe the heart of God would be warmed if his people were free to respond to each other with a few more hugs, embraces, and kisses on the cheek. To respond and greet each other with an enthusiasm that says, "I love you and you're a very special person to me." Perhaps in the full and meaningful responses to one another we can show those without Christ that it is possible to relate to one another other than promiscuously. We can be "free indeed."

7

Free to Be Free

Free to Be Free

Why do some men and women come to accept Christ as their Lord and others reject him? Perhaps, for those who walk away from him, it is because the simple and basic issue has been lost, the water has been muddied. I'm convinced this was the case with one of my fellow students at a local university. I had shared my testimony and had leaned back waiting for his reaction. His reply caught me by surprise.

"Frankly, I'd never become a Christian because as far as I can see Christians are the most neurotic, tied–up kind of people I know."

I admitted the partial truth of his observations and pressed home the claims of Christ rather than the reflections of the Christian community.

"I'm sorry. I just can't buy what you're selling. The people I know who go to church and worship Jesus are worried about the wrong things as far as I'm concerned. They worry about going to movies and playing cards and drinking beer while the world is plagued with poverty, hunger, and injustice. Their value system is too different from mine. I just couldn't play their games."

We talked a few minutes more but the door had been shut. He was convinced that to become a Christian he would have to become bound rather than become free. The invitation wasn't attractive at all. He had accepted a caricature of Jesus Christ as being true and nothing would change his mind.

I wish I could say that his response was an isolated one, but it wasn't. Time after time in my graduate studies I found fellow students and professors to have been turned off not by the person of Christ but by the lives of Christians who supposedly reflect his teachings.

It has been several years since I've attended a class as a graduate student. The intervening years have been taken up mostly with ministry, the ministry of providing therapy and counsel to Christian people whose lives are filled with the hurt and pain of both personal and interpersonal struggles. There is an irony to their struggle. Those who are hurting the most are often the dearest and most committed Christians I know. For some reason, the raw fact of their commitment to Christ has not healed their disease or removed their pain. Their despair is of a kind that wrenches the very commitments they've made. Their despair, I have come to realize, is very much akin to the disbelief of my friends at the university. They are trying to live according to the traditions of Christianity, the same traditions my fellow students at the university were rejecting. In so doing my patients are caught in a terrible bind. They are committed to Jesus Christ as their Lord but the life style they have been taught has bound rather than set them free. Living the Christian life for them has become a nightmare. Somehow the advantages of becoming a Christian haven't yet outweighed the disadvantages, but they can't bring themselves to recant. They're going to remain a Christian even if it kills them.

Counterfeit—or the Real Thing?

For a number of years I found myself defending the Christian life much in the same way I defended my witness at the university. I have since given that up as a lost cause. Some of my fellow therapists in response to the same dilemma, have migrated to a kind of cynicism when it comes to integrating a healthy emotional life with a healthy Christian life. They don't think it can be done. I have been tempted with the same cynicism. The question for those of us who are Christians in the helping professions is whether or not the Christian life is, per se, emotionally and relationally unhealthy. I have become convinced as a Christian professional that the problem lies not with Christ, or the life he offers, but with the distorted view of the Christian life we have been taught. It is the caricature that has robbed us of our freedom and not Christ. The imitation has failed so many of us—not the real thing. If we are to become cynical it should be with the counterfeit life that has been foisted upon us rather than with the reality that Christ offers.

It has been said best by, of all people, the apostle Paul: "For freedom Christ has set us free; stand fast

therefore, and do not submit again to a yoke of slavery"
(Gal. 5:1 RSV).

The apostle struggled in the first century against the
same kind of misinterpretations and misrepresentations
that seem to plague so many of us who are Christians
today. There were those in Galatia who substituted
their rules for the freedom that was inherent in Christ
and Paul rose up, as it were, on his hind legs and
pawed the air against their abuses. He was militant. He
saw in their teachings the insidious nature of their
error. If the Christian life were to be wrapped in the
trappings of their rules and proscriptions, the trappings
would soon become chains and the chains would eventually drive people away from Christ rather than attract
people to him. Errors similar to those that threatened
the Galatian church have, unfortunately, become the
accepted Christian life style of today.

Bond or Free?

The decision we face is like that put forth by the
apostle Paul in Galatians 4:21–31. The Galatian
church could live as children of a bondwoman, Hagar,
or they could live as children of the free woman,
Sarah. They could be bound or they could be free.
They could live according to the rules and laws of
Mount Sinai and be slaves, or they could live according to the liberty of the New Covenant and be free. His
injunction to them was to "cast out the bondwoman"
and to choose to be free. Like Paul, I encourage those
of us who find ourselves bound, to choose to be free, to

cast off the chains that bind us and be "free indeed."

How do you do it? Where do you go to find out what to do? At this juncture, I usually turn with my patients to the Scripture to seek an answer. The passage I most often turn to is found in John's Gospel:

> Jesus then said to the Jews who had believed in him, "If you continue in my word, you are truly my disciples, and you will know the truth, and the truth will make you free." They answered him, "We are descendants of Abraham, and have never been in bondage to any one. How is it that you say, 'You will be made free'?"
>
> Jesus answered them, "Truly, truly, I say to you, everyone who commits sin is a slave to sin. The slave does not continue in the house for ever; the son continues for ever. So if the Son makes you free, you will be free indeed" (John 8:31–36 RSV).

According to Jesus, there is a correlation between truth and freedom. If you are living according to the truth you will be free. If you are bound, it must be because you are living according to error. I would suggest, based on this passage, that there are four ways you can live your life, three of which are products of error and one that is a product of the truth.

The first way you can pattern your life is as a *slave who knows he is a slave and lives as one.* In the time of Christ there were those who were slaves to sin and openly lived as such. They made no pretenses. They were the publicans and sinners of the day. They were estranged both from God and from the religious establishment.

As it was in Christ's day so it is today. There are
those in our world who knowingly and openly live their
lives as if God doesn't exist. The nature of their slavery
may differ. It may be drugs; it may be materialism; it
may be a hundred different things. The end result is an
open and honest rejection of the things of God.

The irony of it all is that Jesus spent much of his
time with people like these. He was their friend (Matt.
11:19), and he offered his kingdom to them (Matt.
9:13). Evidently, as a group, they were comfortable
with him, to the point where several of his earliest
followers came from their ranks (e.g. Matthew and
Mary Magdalene). His invitation today to those who
find themselves to be enslaved is the same as his invitation was to those who were slaves of sin in his day. He
beckons them to come and be healed. In him they will
find rest.

If the publicans and the sinners were slaves to sin
and knew they were, the second category of people
were even worse off. *They were slaves to sin but operated under the false assumption that they were sons of
God.* They were the Pharisees.

Although the Pharisees had an earlier constructive
effect upon the history of the nation of Israel, by the
time of Christ their religious–political system had
hardened into meaningless forms and rituals. They
were a devout people and extremely pious. Their attitudes toward religion had taken on the aura of authority. Because so much of Jesus' behavior did not fit
their proscriptions, the Pharisees were among the leaders in the plot to have Jesus killed according to the

gospel writers. They had allowed the rigid forms of their traditions to be substituted for the heart and soul of the Law.

> And he answered, "You shall love the Lord your God with all your heart, and with all your soul, and with all your strength, and with all your mind; and your neighbor as yourself" (Luke 10:27 RSV).

In substituting their forms and traditions for the heart of the Law, they drew the wrath and ire of Jesus himself as he denounced their empty pious rituals (Cf. Matt. 15:7–11; 23:1–12).

In particular they had become known for four characteristics, each proper in its own right but each cold and valueless when wrapped in the trappings of their tradition.

They were, first of all, extremely zealous for the Law. They strained at interpreting the smallest of issues while at the same time losing sight of the mercy and temperance they were supposedly upholding. They nitpicked the Law to the point where it had lost its dynamic, all with characteristic zeal.

Secondly, because of their emphasis upon the finer points of the Law, they ended up emphasizing externally correct behavior rather than the attitudes of the heart. For example, they became preoccupied with working on the sabbath to the point where they wouldn't allow Jesus to heal a man with a withered hand (Mark 3:2). They became overly concerned with the shell while losing sight of the kernel. What they emphasized wasn't wrong, it was just irrelevant to the greater and broader issues to which Jesus addressed himself. They were externally correct but internally nearsighted.

The third characteristic of their approach to both life and God was their judgmental and corrective attitude toward others. They were always right and others were always wrong. Rarely were their judgments tempered with mercy. Their relationships with their adherents made them appear to be hard and brittle, uncaring and merciless.

Last of all, they were characterized by a separatist approach to life. Separation was the natural extension of their teachings regarding good and evil. According to the Pharisees the way you preserve good is to separate it from evil. You can imagine their horror when Jesus, who claimed to be the Messiah, insisted on eating with sinners. For them, his behavior nullified his claims. He couldn't be from God if he insisted on having the riff–raff of the world as his friends.

The saddest commentary of all was that they falsely assumed their traditions to be of sufficient merit to recommend them to God. They were slaves to sin, not the raucous sins of the publicans, but the subtle and seductive sins of hypocrisy and insincerity.

Modern Pharisees

Unfortunately, there are those today who have patterned themselves after the Pharisees, most often unknowingly. They have substituted form and ritual for the dynamic of faith and love. They are religious to the

150

point of martyrdom but their religiosity is taken up with the preservation of their traditions rather than the heart and soul issues that dominated Jesus' ministry. They falsely assume they are sons of God without ever having experienced the new birth. Theirs is the greatest tragedy of all.

The two previously mentioned ways of living life involve those who are slaves to sin, one knowingly and the other unknowingly. The next way to approach life is of greater concern to me in this chapter because it represents so many in the Christian community who have genuinely committed themselves to Jesus Christ as Lord, yet they have discovered nothing of the privileges of being a child of God. *They are sons of God who are still living as if they are slaves to sin.* All of the characteristics that marked the Pharisees mark them. They are zealous for the Word of God; they are preoccupied with externally correct behavior; they are judgmental of themselves and of others; and they cope with the temptations of life by separating from them and withdrawing into self–contained communities. They are Christians but they are legalists of the first order.

My candid observation is that it is the legalists in the Christian world who portray a caricature of the Christian life that has turned so many people away from the gospel. When it comes to living the Christian life, it is defined in terms of a specific set of traditions, usually in the form of a set of behaviors a "good" Christian doesn't do. The emphasis is upon the negative, the circumscription of behavior. The rules become walls designed to keep the good guys in and the bad guys out. Unfortunately, any definition of the Christian life in terms of negative proscriptions accomplishes just that; it keeps the people who need Christ the most from finding him. It keeps the bad guys out.

Defining the Christian life in terms of negative or legalistic rules and traditions also presents an intolerable problem to some of its most committed followers. What do you do when you are doing all that you're supposed to not be doing and it still isn't working? (That's a cumbersome sentence, but say it to yourself again.) What else do you stop doing? This has been the deep, soul-twisting burden of so many of my patients. They are trying so hard to fit into the traditions, to follow the rules, but as hard as they try, it's never enough. What do you not do next? Sometimes, they try the time–worn tactic of the legalist, separation. However, this time it becomes a psychological form of separation. As they separate from reality, they become psychotic. As they remove themselves from the source of their evil, they remove themselves from themselves—but they have to go crazy to do it.

A psychotic break is the extreme reaction of those who are legalistic in their approaches to the Christian life. There are milder forms of reaction. I have found it useful to think of legalism as coming in two distinct forms, ethical legalism and emotional legalism.

The ethical legalist is the one who copes with the evils in his life by developing rules and regulations, the traditions, for dealing with his ethical behavior. He doesn't drink, or smoke, or attend theaters, or swim in mixed company, or any other rule that his traditions say are evil for him. As is the case with any system of rules, soon most of his attention is taken up with the enforcement of the rules. Rather than becoming preoccupied with the positives of Christian ministry, he becomes preoccupied with the negatives of censorship. The system gives the appearance of having a dynamic but the dynamic is negative instead of positive, and it eventually smothers itself to death.

A second form of legalism is as deadening as is ethical legalism. The interesting phenomenon is that, very often, those who have rebelled against ethical legalism still find themselves to be bound. They are bound by emotional legalism. Let me carefully define what I mean by emotional legalism. Its roots are in the coping mechanisms of religious ethical legalism, but the traditions change from ethical concerns to emotional concerns. The subject matter changes but the object remains the same.

Rather than being preoccupied with a zeal for the Law as was the Pharisee, the emotional legalist often becomes zealous for doing things his, or the "right" way. There's a way things are supposed to be done and, come hell or high water, he is going to see they are done his way. He becomes rigid and is known for his resistance to change. The traditions are no longer ethical but procedural.

The emotional legalist can also be known for his or her emphasis upon the "right" and "proper" behavior. He may have long since broken free of his ethical legalism and have ventured out to the movies. But visit his home and you run into rule stacked upon rule. He might serve wine for dinner but it has to be served in a certain kind of glass, or it has to be a certain brand. If either the glass or the brand of wine isn't right then he feels the whole meal is ruined. He has the freedom to go to the beach for a vacation but if the vacation doesn't go exactly as he planned, the joy is lost completely. If everything isn't "just right," it's all wrong.

The Emotional Legalist

Not until recently was I able to see that at our house I am the emotional legalist, the one who needs the towels in our bathroom hung up not only neatly but evenly, folded in thirds. I am the one who gets upset if our plans for a night out go awry. I am the one who finds it hard to adjust and be flexible to change. All of this tends to make life difficult at times. I find it hard to sit back and relax, free to enjoy the simple things of life. I find myself hurtling through time, busy but never done. It has made me very aware of the times when I am "free." My freedom is like a drink of cool water from a stream when you're desperately thirsty. Much of the joy is being able to sit back and savor its coolness, to be able to pause and be refreshed.

I have also noticed that emotional legalists tend to use other mechanisms characteristic of the Pharisees. They tend to be critical and judgmental of themselves and others. When their rules have been breached they tend to use withdrawal as the means for demonstrating their disapproval. I have known mothers who are emotional legalists to withdraw from their children and not speak to them for days when the child had angered them. And I have heard of husbands who have withdrawn sexually from their wives for weeks because of something the wife has done. Where the Pharisees used separation as a means of isolating good from evil, the emotional legalist uses the withdrawal of approval and affection.

All of this makes the emotional legalist, like the ethical legalist, difficult to live with. As was the case of Pharisaical legalism, the emotional legalist soon finds life to be empty of joy.

In contrast to legalism, Jesus brought joy back into the world rather than taking it away. He began to define life in terms of freedom and liberty. He offered his followers the option to be "free indeed."

The Way We Are Meant to Be

Thus far I have discussed three ways we can live our lives. We can live as slaves to sin who acknowledge they are slaves, we can live as slaves who assume we are sons, and we can live as slaves even though we are in reality sons. The fourth alternative is what I believe Jesus meant when he gave his disciples the opportunity to be "free indeed." *It is possible to be a son who lives as a son.*

Much of the New Testament is taken up with what it means to live the Christian life as a son of God. The early disciples discovered the contrast between the traditions of their day and the freedom they had in Christ. That freedom motivated them to live their lives completely for him. Life, as they came to live it, tasted good. What was it that spurred them on? Why were they able to endure their hardships and deprivations even to the point of martyrdom? They must have discovered a way of life that made it all worthwhile. They had learned to be free even though bound and imprisoned. They were free because they were free inside.

I'd like to suggest that there were at least two principles that came to dominate each of the early disciples who learned to be "free indeed." If those of us who are bound can grasp and apply these principles to our lives, perhaps we, too, like the early disciples, will learn to be free inside.

To begin with, they came to accept, believe, and live as forgiven men and women. Where once they had lived under the pale of judgment and condemnation, in Christ they learned to live as forgiven people. Paul's Christian journey began in Romans 7 where he cried, "Wretched man that I am! Who will set me free from this body of death?" (Rom. 7:24 RSV). It ended in Romans 8 where he exulted, "There is therefore now no condemnation for those who are in Christ Jesus" (Rom. 8: 1 RSV). The journey for the early disciples was from the judgment of death to the joy of forgiveness.

For those of us who are modern–day legalists, both ethical and emotional, the application is obvious. It just doesn't make sense for us to go on living critically of ourselves and of others, insisting on our own way,

---

when the God of the universe has forgiven us. How can we possibly justify doing that to ourselves and to others when the One who has every right to judge no longer does so because of Jesus Christ?

I am reminded of the example of Jesus recorded in John 8:1–11. He was confronted with a dilemma by the Pharisees. Should he uphold the traditions of the "law" which taught that the woman taken in adultery should be stoned to death, or should he set her free in defiance of the law? His accusers waited for him to act. They thought they had him cornered. His response provides us with a clear example of how the tension between the rules and traditions of life can be met without doing violence to either the rules or to the rule breaker.

First of all, he took his time before he acted. His response wasn't impulsive. It was deliberate. Secondly, he reminded her accusers that none of them was free from sin, each of them had broken the law and was likewise guilty. No one goes through life without breaking the rules. To be reminded of this fact is to remember that justice must always be tempered with mercy. Thirdly, when it came to the application of the law, he focused upon the spirit of the law rather than the letter. The letter would have seen her killed, but the spirit took her repentant heart into account. He was able to maintain the integrity of the law by applying it justly. Had he applied it legalistically the rules would have been served but the person would have been ground up in the process. People are always more important than rules. And last of all, he gave her another chance, the opportunity to change. Legalism, when it condemns, tends to condemn forever. Jesus acted, forgave her, and sent her on her way. Her ordeal was over. Because he forgave she could forget. Compassion, tolerance, and forgiveness: the marks of a free man, one who is "free indeed."

Free to Surrender

The second principle that came to dominate the early disciples who were "free indeed" seems on the surface to be a paradox. The disciples became truly free because they were free to surrender their freedom. It was this discipline that protected against the abuse of their freedom. While Christ had made them "free indeed," they were still his by way of his Lordship. Using Paul's analogy, they were to be a "living sacrifice" (Rom. 12:1). They were no longer their own, they had been bought with a price. Based upon their commitment to him, their behavior took on a new dimension. They lived their lives in light of the Lordship of Christ, a relationship that makes lists of rules superfluous.

A further dimension of this second principle was touched upon by Jesus. It is recorded in John's Gospel:

> No longer do I call you servants, for the servant does not know what his master is doing; but I have called you friends, for all that I have heard from my Father I have made known to you. You did not choose me, but I chose you and appointed you that you should go and bear fruit and that your fruit should abide; so that

whatever you ask the Father in my name, he may give
it to you. This I command you, to love one another
(John 15:15–17 RSV).

The disciples were no longer slaves, they were friends.
They were meant by the Lord Jesus to enjoy the
privilege of their position. They had access to his
Father in the same way he had access. Their privileges
were such that they would never again be slaves.

Verse 17 of this passage summarized their responsibilities to one another and it has become the greatest of
the commandments for the Christian. "This I command you, to love one another." It is this commandment that takes the place of the legalist's rules and
traditions. It is this commandment that establishes the
conditions to make any form of legalism, whether
ethical or emotional, irrelevant and useless. The believer in Jesus Christ is to follow Jesus' example and to
relate to his fellow man in love, the commitment to
seek and to act in the best interest of others. The
freedom to surrender your freedom ultimately defines
your relationship to others in terms of love.

In writing this chapter, I have had some goals. I
have wanted to examine the traditions in our Christian
faith that have tended to make the offer of new life in
Christ both unattractive to many observant unbeliev-
ers, and difficult to follow in the case of many of our
most committed brothers and sisters in Christ. The
traditions of ethical legalism have robbed us of the joy
and attractiveness of the Christian life. Even more
subtle, however, is the impact of a second kind of
legalism, emotional legalism. It has robbed even more

of us of our freedoms because it does so with such cunning thoroughness that we lose the joy of living without knowing it is gone. The zest for life in general and the zest for the Christian life evaporates under the weight of self–imposed regulations making the mere fact of living a burden.

If I have said anything, I have wanted to say that in Christ the true joy of living returns. I'm convinced that most of us in the Christian world have never fully tasted what is rightfully ours in Christ. We stumble along in the dust and dirt of life while Christ bids us come fly with the eagles. We wallow in the misery of slavery rather than bask in the privileges of our sonship. In closing, I would remind you of Paul's definition of what it means to be "free indeed":

"For freedom Christ has set us free; stand fast therefore, and do not submit again to a yoke of slavery" (Gal. 5:1).

Only in Christ are we truly free to be "free indeed."